The Quest for the Fine

The Quest for the Fine

A Philosophical Inquiry
into Judgment, Worth, and Existence

by
Michael Gelven

Rowman & Littlefield Publishers, Inc.

ROWMAN & LITTLEFIELD PUBLISHERS, INC.

Published in the United States of America
by Rowman & Littlefield Publishers, Inc.
4720 Boston Way, Lanham, Maryland 20706

3 Henrietta Street
London, WC2E 8LU, England

Copyright © 1996 by Rowman & Littlefield Publishers, Inc.

All rights reserved. No part of this publication may be
reproduced, stored in a retrieval system, or transmitted
in any form or by any means, electronic, mechanical,
photocopying, recording, or otherwise, without the prior
permission of the publisher.

British Cataloging in Publication Information Available

Library of Congress Cataloging-in-Publication Data

Gelven, Michael.
The quest for the fine : a philosophical inquiry into judgment, worth,
and existence / by Michael Gelven.
p.   cm.
Includes bibliographical references and index.
1. Philosophical anthropology. I. Title.
BD450.G443   1995   121'.8–dc20   95-37357

ISBN 0–8476–8123–8 (cloth : alk. paper)
ISBN 0–8476–8124–6 (pbk.: alk. paper)

Printed in the United States of America

   The paper used in this publication meets the minimum requirements of
the American National Standard for Information Sciences—Permanence
of Paper for Printed Library Materials, ANSI Z39.48–1984.

To
Todd Kukla and Sharon Sytsma

Contents

Acknowledgments		ix
Introduction		xi
1	Refined Perception	1
2	Perceived Essence	19
3	The Aesthetics of the Fine	37
4	Becoming Fine	49
5	The Gracious	63
6	The Common	79
7	Fine Truth	89
8	Transformation	105
9	The Wretched	115
10	Judgment	127
11	The Philosopher as Fine	139
Index		157
About the Author		167

Acknowledgments

This book was written with the grants and released time that accompanied awarding of the Presidential Research Professorship in Philosophy at Northern Illinois University in 1993. I am grateful for this honor and the assistance that comes with it. I am also indebted to those whose ready ear and discerning criticism in the current of philosophical sharing inspired and emboldened: to Dr. Fran Mayeski, my sister, for bearing with my complaints; to Professor Donald Livingston for his criticisms of the manuscript; to Dr. Herman Stark, who read my work with generosity and favor; and to those students who make it such a joy to share with them—especially Adam Biesterfeld, Dmitri Peskov, Troy Cross, and Chris Morgan.

Introduction

> young boys and girls
> Are level now with men: the odds is gone,
> And there is nothing left remarkable
> Beneath the visiting moon.
>
> —*Antony and Cleopatra*

It is a singular mark of the fine that it is often fully realized only in its loss. It is not merely that we become numbed by custom and familiarity; it is rather that the supremely fine seems knotted to our finitude, that even when held most dear, it is made more precious by the frail deed of our ownership. When the wondrous Cleopatra holds Antony's unspirited corpse in her arms, the cry befits her royalty; for only fine language reveals the fine. It is magnificent grief, for the pain is fused into a single, dread realization of a bitter, radiant truth. What is most unbearable to Egypt's queen in the loss of her beloved is the bleak sameness that is left behind.

Where nothing is remarkable there is neither royalty nor royal love, perhaps no love at all. The terrible evening out of things makes all things worthless; the even eclipses the odds, there is no real risk; the lottery is but a child's game. That there should be no difference between a great warrior and a playground of equal children is a fatal thought, and Cleopatra's end is sounded by the simple sound of it. Yet her lament echoes the realization that the wonderful is sometimes but a guest. The moon visits; it does not abide. Perhaps all that matters is fleeting; it is only the same that drearily remains the same. The fine triumphs, however briefly, against the dread nihilism of equal sameness that stretches smoothly on forever like the arid plain on a desolate, forgotten landscape. This is not a prejudice of the princely over the common, but a universal grasp of a truth that conjoins our reality with how we think. The fine can be lost like youth. Yet, the poetry that sustains is the finest, and it abides forever.

Why "fine"? We speak of their finest hour, meaning the most noble and splendid moment in their history; of a fine wine, which is not only excellent but carefully aged and unbruised by clumsy handling; of a fine young man, meaning he holds promise of a high achievement and is mannerly, handsome, and respectful; of a fine machine, meaning well crafted and robustly capable of delicate but powerful work; of a fine day, meaning that it is beautiful and deserving of our attention and memory; of a fine angler, pianist, or ballerina, meaning practiced and graceful, with an achieved elegance; of a fine nib of a pen, meaning narrow, thin, precise; of a fine point, meaning subtle but significant, a delicacy that conquers by precision and clarity; of fine gold, which means pure, unalloyed, not mixed with baser metal; of the fine arts, as opposed to the practical, not needing utility to justify it. Its etymological origins, however, are closer to that which is finished, final, finite, even dead. To pay a fine is to put an end to the legal matter; the antique phrase "in fine" means to bring to an end. Precisely because it is the final or the last, it is thereby thought to be supremely precious, the goal or purpose of all endeavors like the Aristotelean telos. Its precision lies in its finitude—its finishing or completeness.

If the meanings of this word are so dispersed across the lexical atlas, why not select a less-wanton term such as beautiful, great, excellent, or noble? The answer is, in part, because among the learned these terms have become mere labels, and are already freighted with the baggage of so much analysis they cease to be a source of understanding and instead become that which needs to be understood. Further, there is a pervading sense in most uses of the term that the fine is achieved partly by refinement; and in this sense, it weighs against the merely natural gifts of the fortuitously lovely. Refinement suggests careful working and reworking, building on what has come before, hence, an historical development enhanced by learning and guildry, leading toward mastery, the way centuries hone a language to poetic power; or cultivation, and not merely natural selection, enriches a civilization. Cleopatra's words reflect a refined genius: the fine becomes a concrete bulwark against reductionism with regard to meaning; it is a weir against the appalling torrent of sterile, nihilistic sameness. Explanations that reduce all to the same create not a synthesizing principle by which the differences can be thought, but an anesthesia and numbness in which the multitude of identical sand grains displays a Sahara of unlimited and hence unthinkable equality. On such endless, indifferent sweeps, Cleopatra, and all that is meaningful, becomes irrelevant.

The fine surpasses mere refinement, however, as Wagner so eloquently shows us in *The Master-Singers of Nuremburg*; a mere pedant of refinement like Beckmesser is as inimical to the fine as the gifted tyro Walter whose creativity is marred by a lack of learned discipline—a piece of artistic wisdom that inspires Nietzsche's marriage of the Apollonian with the Dionysian. Refinement prepares for true creative genius and wedding them procreates the fine.

The fine is a nomad among the shelters of thought; it is not restricted to the arts, nor to morality or goodness, nor to social improvement, not even to metaphysics, though it pervades all of these. Like the Greek term *kalos*, the fine is beautiful, good, noble, excellent, and refined; yet it is more than any of these, more even than all put together. It is precisely this diverse unification among the disciplines that gives it its rarely recognized rank; it is a great unifying phenomenon, not an abstract maxim, pervading all the disciplines from the mathematician's native inclination to elegance to the philosopher's adherence to Ockham's razor and the artist's instinct for simplicity. Thus, beauty, in the sense of refined elegance, is one of the persistent meanings that pervades the quest for the fine, though we cannot equate the two terms. We must inquire into what being beautiful means to help us on the quest, but we are misled down alleyways of distraction if we seek the fine only among the beautiful. We need distinctions between the disciplines, but not exclusivity.

That there is danger in this knightly quest is palpable. If these brief reflections on Cleopatra's lament are fertile, we have already seen some perils of the search. Why should the fine await its loss to be realized? Is this not a tragic destiny of the quest? Why is it a greater misfortune to be reduced to nihilistic sameness in which all is safe and risk is gone? Is not the nomadic insecurity of the fine a reason to disregard it and seek more familiar and more stable treasures? Why embark on this quest at all?

The embarkation is compelled because as Cleopatra learns at the passing of Antony, the absence of the fine entails nihilism. Nihilism denies meaning. In the technical, philosophical sense, it denies there is any way our reasoning, experience, or thinking can ever produce a single thought, argument, or confirmation that anything matters at all. It need not be skeptical, since the nihilist may agree we have great quantities of knowledge; nor need it even be relativistic, since he may be quite willing to assert and affirm it is wrong to betray the trustful or abuse the child, or, unlike the anarchist, to destroy the civilization. The nihilist may admit these but simply denies that they are meaningful; that although two plus two really does equal four, it does not matter that it does or even that we know it does. This locates the quest in the realm of meaning, so that the prevailing form of the question becomes "What does it mean to be fine?" We set out on the quest because truth matters, even secretive, shy, gossamer-fine truth—truth that is not reducible to factual assertions or logical formulae; truth that reveals what it means to be who and what we are; yet, truth that must be approached critically and with much experience, reflection, and argumentation, so that the quest remains steadfast to Plato's teaching that truth and opinion are distinctly different, entirely different, and not at all the same.

A quest, especially in the knightly sense, is always tentative, beguiled by the ephemeral, alluring in its promise of complete sanctity and treasure, a perilous journey after the Holy Grail, noble in its purpose but curiously sad in its inevitable frustration, even as it is infinitely rich in its route. A quest is not a proof nor a thesis, though it must, since it is truth directed, constitute an argument; the knight does not seek the grail to take possession of it but to be possessed by it, not to end the search but to validate it.

To insist, in knightly fashion, that the paradox is itself truth bearing, that the fine may be the way to truth, reminds us of Plato, who teaches that only the most excellent is real, that the perfect forms give meaning and reality to the fleeting instances of our experience even though such forms ever evade our mortal grasp. It perhaps also reminds us of Heidegger's wisdom, that to be at all is intelligible only because we can succeed or fail at it, that existence is authentic or inauthentic; but this is lofty heritage indeed. If such rare thinkers, in their rarity and greatness, embrace this paradox, why should it deter us?

We seek what it means to be fine, for in learning this we learn wisdom, which is reverence for truth just because it is true. If there is a paradox in this, we learn the paradox, seeking the truth imbedded there, for that is the quest. It is the quest itself that unfolds the truth inherent in the paradox; it is not an adherence to a doctrine beyond any questioning; indeed, it is not an orthodoxy at all. Truth can never be so corralled.

It is not enough to unfetter differences from the shackles of the same, as if making distinctions were to uncover truth simply by the divisions; nor does it suffice to develop an elitist disdain for what is constant. It is not the different that matters, but the fine; the "same" here is not the abiding magnificence of the universal, but the fearsome tyranny of common thought—curiously antiuniversal—that all opinions are equal, that boys and girls are even now with men.

The quest for the fine is a species of philosophical inquiry, metaphoric of a journey through a wilderness of envious lands with shibboleths as names, resisting intrusion to all but the steadfast, well-trained, crack troops of the fighting elite. The enemy here is not merely ignorance, which perhaps the common infantry could battle, but muddled thinking and confusion, far greater foes to truth than simple error. If the quest is for truth and not merely refined pleasure or sophisticated manners, important as these may be, the metaphor of the knightly warrior is more than apt, for the critical dedication must persist throughout all trials, keen to the awareness that the grail in this case is indeed holy—truth itself!—and not to be abandoned when the way becomes tangled or the perils seductive.

Chief among these perils is the enigma of the very first mile to be trekked. We appreciate or at least appraise the fine; it is a matter of judgment. However, the appreciated need not be the true; one seems entirely personal, the other independent. It seems that the fine is precisely that which is an afterthought to the solid and significant, as if truth itself were rude and basic, like simple food, unadorned by sauce or garnish, whereas the fine is merely what we add to give it flavor, containing no nourishment in itself. There is at least a paradox in this. The fine must be shown to be essential and not merely decorative, truthful and not merely attractive; yet, if it be rare and remarkable, we seem to sequester it from the obvious and trustworthy, making the quest appear a skeptic's delight, mowing the lawn of belief, leaving only the grit of doubt like clippings of grass. But reflection assures us that the fine is neither decorative, inessential, nor skeptical. It is not our search for the fine that demeans the common, but the common that demeans the search. It is not skeptical but cautious; it does not mistrust what is plain but refines it to reveal its essence, as plain truth often startles when denuded. This does not entirely defuse the sputtering paradox, for the unease at the possible explosion remains: is not finery judgmental, and being so, is it not inessential?

Judgment is not mere opinion, but neither is it certainty. Indeed, it is the very judgmental character of the fine that paradoxically reveals what is essential, so that essence is available only through judgment. In this we turn the paradox on its head to make it a friend and not a threat to truth. If we can show that only through judgment can the fine be achieved, and only through refinement can essence be realized, the judgmental character of the fine need not distress, though it still vexes. The quest, after all, is not for the certain but for the seeker.

There is another facet to this paradox. The sage of Oklahoma said he never met a man he didn't like. This seems to speak of a rather charming disposition, a man ready to accept all kinds of human folly with affection. Suppose a contemporary were to say that Will Rogers likes him. So what? Apparently he likes everybody, so that being liked by Will Rogers is not remarkable at all; indeed, as long as one qualifies as human there is a guarantee of his friendship. Saint and sinner, villain and cheat, dull and witty—all are liked. Being liked by this droll westerner seems not to matter at all. Like a whore's pleasure, it is cheapened by its ubiquity.

But we pause at this, as well we might. Somehow the warm but biting camaraderie of Rogers has been altered by this critique into precisely that dread sameness that haunts the grieving Cleopatra. Can this be what the cowboy meant to say? Reflection on this gentle humorist's most famous remark seems to darken it, distort it, even press it beyond what was meant. If such is the rapine of this quest, perhaps it is better not to reflect at all. Yet, like a misswallowed morsel that chokes, it will not go down. If the fine reveals essence, and each of us has our own essence, then it would seem that the fine is entirely common, available to all, and, hence, without luster.

Argumentation based on paradox thwarts these simplistic reductions; we are always pulled back to our basic confrontations even as the speculative may dazzle. There are the rude and the refined, those who speak well and those who speak badly, those who dine and those who devour. The interest here is not in sociological classification or even moral contempt for the wretched deprived of refinement. We need not look to others but within ourselves, for we know that both the vulgar and the exquisite are possibilities that can never be entirely shunned. Perhaps contempt for the vulgar is justified, but if so, it is always our own vulgarity challenged by our own contempt. It is supremely foolish to deny there are those who are base and those who are noble; but if we do not deny either the possibilities or the actual people who embody them, what are we to do with this realization? How are we to think about the crass and the fine? How may this very distinction enable us to think in certain ways denied us were we not to make the distinction? How may it enable us to think at all? If it is possible to be both fine and vulgar, what does this tell us about ourselves?

To address these questions requires a kind of refinement. We must first learn to refine our own capacity to perceive the fine, and only then to achieve it. This may seem like a curious approach, for it suggests that perceiving itself is something we can do well or badly, and that it can be enhanced by a kind of training or erudition. It may seem that perceiving does not permit degrees—we either see or do not see—and, hence, refinement has nothing to do with it. Further, it suggests that perceiving is not merely a passive reception of stimuli—a hideous phrase—but is controlled, active, and learned. In any event, this knightly quest must begin here with the raising of the question: What does it mean to perceive finely what is fine?

Chapter 1

Refined Perception

She speaks razors. Yet, though the cuts are painful, her graciousness soothes like a balm. Her stiletto words pierce deeply, perhaps even fatally; but the generosity of her truth salves the wound by sacrifice. In one of her most penetrating lines we hear:

> Because I could not stop for Death—
> He kindly stopped for me—
> The Carriage held but just Ourselves
> And Immortality.

The passage is beautiful, as is the entire poem; but one word stands out with unexpected and cruel power. A poet does not write, but speaks; and in this discourse, the poet, Emily Dickinson, recasts our entire universe with one, single, devastating word that we cannot forget even were we to try. This word is kindly. With that fine and solitary word we are entirely remade; for the beam of death is now refracted through the poet's prism disarming it of its terror. For what could it possibly mean to speak of our mortality as a kindness?

We may, of course, dismiss this, self-deceptively, by hearing in it a peculiar death wish of one fatigued by life, seeking the final requiescat of the grave. We may abuse it by hearing irony, sarcasm, or even nihilism in the poet's apparent eagerness to die; or we may dismiss it as a naive trust in a romantic afterlife. These responses are to label it, putting it on some unreachable shelf for eternally delayed revisitation. Labels remove all need to think; they classify what would be thought into "ideas," singular opinions of a specially perverse class that are different than our own and, hence, mere objects of bemused interest. But, such hearing is unworthy of what she speaks.

From the first line, we hear she was unwilling to stop for death—hence, hers is no death wish or nihilistic ennui; she does not choose to die, but, having death confront her, she unexpectedly recognizes in it a kindness. Perhaps the kindness lies precisely in not having to select death or life, but in accepting both as necessary parts of our fundamental essence as mortal. She is not eager for death since she "would not stop" for it, but sees in its inevitability a carriage of her destiny. If we learn to look upon our fate as distinctly our own, then, that we are mortal may be ultimately embraced as a kindness; and this is remarkable even as it is universally precious to each of us. She speaks further, telling us the carriage driver "knew no haste"; so the slowly driven journey is not about death, but about life as she passes children playing in the ring and fields of what she calls "Gazing Grain." This is an odd locution indeed, suggesting the grain gazes at us, not that we gaze at it, though we almost lose this by mishearing "grazing"—a species of homophonic amphiboly she uses often throughout her works. The poem's final metaphor of the grave as a near-buried house suggests a home, where we belong at journey's end, an image that gives pith and meaning to the earlier, remarkable "kindly." Dickinson is a poet of the single word, as Keats is of the line and Auden of the phrase and Shakespeare of them all. With her magic, she releases the power of an island-word, a lonely, volcanic thrust from the endless sea establishing an entirely fresh girded land, that gives us new anchorage. In this poetic phenomenon, in which a single ordinary word takes on spectacular revelatory power, we find the first indication of what fine language actually performs. If we probe just a little deeper, we may ask what is revealed by these remarkable spotlights on single everyday words, orphaned by the poet's genius from their security in the hiddenness of prose into unrobed, radiant disclosures? What is disclosed, what is revealed? It is not a fact, an idea, or an interpretation. It is rather an essence. We are in essence mortal, and in the startling revelation of this, we discover that though death may be dreaded, it is necessarily ours, and it belongs to us, as families do; or we belong to it as we do to fretful siblings, in whose anomalous return there is a species of kindliness known as welcome, however reluctant.

These are familiar phenomena. Many fine lines in poetry evoke a sense that the selection of the terms is so remarkable that no other term suffices. A Mozart melody also seems perfect, as if discovered rather than created, each note in its proper place, instantly familiar and entirely breathtaking. Yet, though these artistic phenomena are undeniable, the underlying supports (or presuppositions) are disturbing. If we say that Dickinson has selected the perfect word or Mozart the perfect note, the suggestion is that there is an essence to be isolated. For what is it that makes these gifted selections recognized as uniquely revealing? It can only mean that not all words or notes are equal, but that what is revealed is not how we happen to think about it but how we must think about it. How we must think about something is its essence.

By this move, we place the issue on far more serious and demanding grounds; it is not the beauty of the word that penetrates, but the *fineness* of it, for it is the fine that directs us to the essence. The fine may be beautiful but not all beauty is fine. The demands of the quest require eventual analysis of these key terms, *beauty* and *essence*. For the moment, the emphasis is on the emerging maxim that the fine perceived reveals essences—that in our perception of the fine, we learn what it means for the perceived to be what it is in truth—not a representation floating unanchored in our consciousness. This emphasis focuses on the fine as the sharp and penetrative, which, in its precision, allows for depth in probing, like a hypodermic needle; and with this simile, it is somewhat easier to realize why only the fine pierces deeply enough to enter the inner secrets. A blunt syringe does not penetrate as smoothly or even, perhaps, as deeply as a fine, sharp one.

The simile is at best an aid; it is not an argument. Why do we say it is the *fineness* of the language rather than its beauty that reveals the essence? The selection of Dickinson's poem is carefully made, for much beautiful and even great poetry does not turn on the isolation of a single, stunning term as this poem does. Attention is drawn to the single word "kindly" as an instance of a particularly fine selection, where the listener feels only this one word will do, and that what this word does is remarkable. The fine as perceived, therefore, establishes rank, which beauty need not always do; it also is something achieved, usually through careful refinement, but, more rarely, through the spontaneous generosity of genius. Its peculiar power is that it penetrates into the very core of things—which means there must *be* the very core, and not many possible cores, subjectively selected to satisfy our private perspectives. There is, then, at the very least, resistance to a relativism of meaning that would persuade us that phenomena are meaningful to me because of how I react, and meaningful to you in possibly different ways because of how you react. Such a view is now challenged. If there is a perfect word or note and if that perfection reveals the essence (and not merely one among many essences—that is an absurdity), then the refinement of the fine is not relative to different subjects or even to different cultures but simply true. The image of the apprentice in the guild refining his skills and his judgment under the guidance of a master reinforces this essentialist understanding.

To perceive in Dickinson's poem how to think about our own reality as mortal, challenges our normal understanding both of our mortality and of perception itself. We are first surprised not only that death can be friendly, but also that as a part of our essence, it necessarily must be so. We are also shocked to learn that to perceive—in this case to hear—seems to entail a species of thinking—the thinking that penetrates into the essence. This strikes us as odd since we have long since learned from philosophers that perception is entirely distinct from thinking, that the former is empirical and, hence, contingent, the latter is rational and, hence, lawlike or necessary. It is further disturbing to realize that perceiving itself can be refined—that we can succeed and fail in varying degrees at perceiving. This challenges the rather common notion that perception is a simple given, that is: we either perceive or do not perceive. We must be trained to perceive finely; fine perceiving is achieved through refinement.

These cursory reflections must now be anchored in firmer analyses, for there is much at stake here that goes beyond the mere appreciation of a keen poet's insight. Our first refinement must be on the very nature and meaning of perception. So we ask three questions (1) What does it mean to perceive? (2) What does it mean to be enabled by our receptivity? and (3) What does enabled perception mean in art?

What Does It Mean to Perceive?

The formulation of this question, what does it mean to perceive, is important, for the focus here is not on the mechanics of how we perceive, nor on its epistemic dubiety and reliability. We are perceiving beings, sometimes reliably and other times not—a truth that is in itself not in dispute. The practical and valid concern as to how and when our perceptions are trustworthy is one of great and legitimate philosophical interest; but it is not the only question that can be asked. What it means to hear and see and feel is also a legitimate question and may indeed even be the fundamental one, the one that ought to be asked as the most important and the most profound; the one that is always being assumed by all other questions about perception. How can we ask whether perception can give knowledge unless we first know what it means to perceive? It is, in any event, our question and should be addressed critically.

From the reflective wisdom in our tradition, we learn that one compelling account of what it means to perceive is to receive from our environment the signals or tokens that put us in touch with the world. In Plato's *Theaetetus*, for example, one suggestion by the interlocutors is that perception is like a soft tablet onto which various impressions are made, as a signet ring makes its sign when pressed into melted wax. In the dialogue, this account eventually fails as a description of knowledge, but it is easy to see why it is attractive as a suggestion about perception. Centuries after Plato, John Locke resurrects the notion in terms of the *tabula rasa*; and even Immanuel Kant characterizes the first of the three major faculties of the mind as the sensibility, which he argues is a receptive agency. Given such noble support, it is churlish indeed to dismiss this suggestion without reflection. It seems to make a good deal of sense, for we are in the world, which seems far greater than our own unique subjects, and we seem to receive from this world various kinds of information about it through the receptors we call our senses. Since we are not now asking the epistemological question as to whether such perception is sufficient or necessary for knowledge, we can focus more easily on the notion that to perceive is simply to receive; that is, as perceivers we are receptive. It is to emphasize this receptive dimension to our perceiving that Hume designates the primary form of being conscious as an impression.

What does this mean? To be impressed by stimuli suggests an entirely passive role; to receive seems to entail a kind of vacancy or emptiness that, through experience, is thereby filled as an empty bucket is filled by water. Are these metaphors of total passivity—the blank slate, the empty bucket, or the soft wax—sufficient? What does it mean to receive?

The danger here lies in the overly mechanistic image of receiving that these metaphors suggest, as if receiving is entirely reducible to what is received. To be receptive is by no means to be a mere dustbin for the wanton trash thrown in disinterestedly by the sheer randomness of some external bombardment. When we reflect upon what it means to receive, we recognize greater possible modalities than the pelted dartboard of the submissive receptor. It is possible to receive in such a way as to enable, as vision enables our locomotion and action to be less perilous and more controlled; as hearing enables us to learn through discourse the wider experience of others. We call this a species of utilitarian or even pragmatic enablement, which generously expands the range of our safety and experience, and even enriches the quality of life. Through this enabling perception we also become less dependent, freer from guile, and more quickly cognizant of the world we live in; with our eyes working, we can see to pluck the fruit and kill the game, find our mate and guard our children. To be enabled by the reception of these and other perceptions is above all useful and thus liberating. Hence, to perceive is not only to receive but in receiving to be enabled. Yet, the receptivity of perception is not restricted to these practical concerns, important as they are. Another way to receive is to be grateful, for example, as if the reception were of a bestowal; we may also receive duly, as when a reward is given for an achievement, or even receive by right, as a wage, which is neither bestowed nor awarded but earned by dint of labor and contract. For a bucket to receive water is in fact a phenomenon described metaphorically—for buckets do not literally receive, their meaning is exhausted by their utility, and, hence, they are merely filled. The notion of reception cannot be reduced to being filled, impressed by signets, or marked on slates.

Further, there is much to be learned from the submissive aspect to reception, the way one submits to and receives the blows of punishment or torment, that is, entirely as a mute slave or dumb beast or even an insensible object like a rug being beaten for cleanliness. However, we can submit more nobly, as when we submit to the unwelcome demands of our children, or when we submit to the lures of love or the harsh commands of duty. Above all, we can and do submit to the thrall of the fine and the beautiful, as great art makes its demands on us simply because we receive it. This does not in any way deny that perception is both receptive and submissive; it merely expands the range of what these modes mean. Both terms are originally about ways we exist, and only derivatively about purely physical objects made intelligible by a metaphor illuminating the application of mechanistic laws.

Thus, to be able to receive as enabling—that is, to perceive—requires far more than the material image of being peppered randomly by activations of sensory organs. We must ask about perception as enabling—that is, how we, in the mode of submission and receptivity are freed from the mere mechanistic accounts of prior and posterior events connected by the vague principle of cause. To be receptive is therefore to make possible being impressed or influenced and not merely *that* we are, as Martin Heidegger points out in *Kant and the Problem of Metaphysics*. Accordingly, being receptive is not fundamentally passive but modally active. The enabling receptivity of perception makes possible a remarkable range of existential modalities, from submission, to adjusting because of ocular evidence, to yielding to the demands of the honored and revered. To be receptive as perceivers is far from passive acceptance; it is the opening up of possibilities that do not merely make it easier for us to function, as if what we perceive is merely instrumental to the achievement of some preperceptual interest. Rather, in the enabling provided by perception, our receptivity makes possible the enlargement of the phenomenon of being learners in the world. It is precisely in this enabling of possibilities that to distinguish the fine from the coarse penetrates the essence.

Yet, the receptive and, hence, enabling submission that characterizes our perception is never originary. The fierce bleating of the vexatious lawn mower early on Sunday mornings or the incessant yipping throughout the night by the neighbor's dog defiles our receptivity entirely against our will. We do not control what we perceive, and often admit that we had as lief avoid witnessing the gruesome accident. It is this very lack of selectivity in our sensing that anchors us in the adventurous world, where fate and fortune bestow both suffering and enlightenment in the endless stream of intrusions beyond our ken. We may select to hear a concert, but hear the roar of the jet overhead; select to witness a sunset and see a polluted reminder of our waste instead. Even when we succeed in achieving what we select to witness, the subservience of our perception is often stunning, as we freely watch a performance of a play that wrangles our sensibility either loftily or basely. Thus, we cannot always, or even usually, determine what we perceive; yet this does not forfeit the variety of ways we can accept or reject our perceptions, either pragmatically, duly, by right, or as grateful. The extent to which we can be grateful or resentful of the same perceived phenomenon, shows that our being receptive is not a mere determined mechanism, but something at which we can succeed or fail, something that is, which is either fine or coarse.

We must delay the loud and persistent knocking on the doors of our discourse demanding consideration of the central theme about essence. It is first required that the range of the modal possibilities shows us that to perceive is no simple answer to anything, but itself is a complex problem. It is granted that our present concern with perception is solely that of its enablement to probe to the essence of things, as is Dickinson's inspired selection of a word, the perception of which is such a powerful penetration into our own essence as mortal—that is, our submission to what it means to be going to die. To raise this question directly without first exploring the pathoempirical meaning of perception as enabling receptivity would err by impatience—a violation, in other words, of the apprentice status of these early probings, and, hence, an offense against the guild of thought.

To perceive, we say, is to receive in an enabling way; it is to be enabled by our receptivity. Such enabling receptivity permits many modal variants, such as the enablement of utility, of gratitude, of right, and of enlightenment. At the same time, perception as enabling reception also means submission, which itself can be either base or noble. Accordingly, what it means to perceive is already shown to be a rich phenomenon fully deserving of considerable analysis. It is enough for us to point to the possibilities, for we are not here required to dig as deeply as the issue deserves; we are concerned solely with the task of understanding how perception itself can be fine, which is to say how perception can pierce into essential meaning as our hearing of Dickinson's poem does. To proceed along these lines, we now must ask a second question.

What Does It Mean to be Enabled by Our Receptivity?

To submit receptively when we perceive is to enable and to expand our existence by learning through the authority inherent in perception. Thus, when I expect the river to yield to the thrusts of my canoe and find the cold has stiffened the water, barring my progress, the sheer experiential power of being arrested by the unexpected solid ice compels submission. Though I thought the water was and would remain fluid and, hence, passable, I am completely thwarted by the reception of this new evidence, and am enabled perforce—that is, I must become able now—to accept that cold turns passable water into impassable ice. This learning, though harsh, enables by enriching my being alert to the world, just as much as vision enables me to walk through a delicate glassware boutique without knocking down costly items.

It is the irresistible nature of such enabling receptivity that is so compelling. When the blinded Gloucester in *King Lear* stumbles piteously across the stage in his newly deprived state, we learn what it means to become sightless. This mere loss, however, is not alone what impresses; for each of us can experiment with such misfortune simply by closing our eyes and trying to move about a familiar room. After knocking our shins on unexpected protuberances, we achieve some vague sense of how enabling the perception provided by vision truly is.

This common frustration is far surpassed by the genius of Shakespeare. We ourselves witness the old man walking on even ground but believing with some reluctance that he is climbing a steep hill simply because his disguised son tells him he climbs. There is pity here in his beguilement, in his submission to the remaining faculties that now mislead. We realize that the blinded Gloucester, once a noble and revered duke, must now submit to the ignominy of relying solely on the testimony of a putative madman; but the enablement does not end here. Edgar stops his blinded father, telling him he is on the very brink of a fearsome cliff. As the son brilliantly describes the vision to his father, the audience, fully aware of the deceit, nevertheless senses the dreadful vertigo of looking down from appalling heights. Entirely against the powerful evidence of our own ocular sense that Gloucester is standing on perfectly even ground, we feel and submit to the vertiginous eloquence of the spoken passage that would convince us there is a cliff there and that Gloucester's demise is but a footfall away. We may, of course, dismiss this merely as the power of poetic genius to focus on what we hear rather than what we see; but there is much more. Even when we see it, the blindness of Gloucester is translated into our own visceral mistrust of what we see, lured by the eloquence of what we hear in Edgar's deceit. The tumbling of Gloucester cheating his death leaves him bewildered and—note this!—more deeply submissive now to his cruel fate. So this we think is what it means to see; this is what it means to hear; this is what it means to submit. The trick by Edgar was meant to redeem his father from unholy despair; but in truth it redeems us, by enabling our senses not to show us the environment but to show us ourselves. This turns our receptivity to our own being receptive—we perceive what it means to perceive. It is this turning of perception—and not conceptual reflection—on itself that enables us to penetrate to essential meaning. But how can we perceive our own perceiving? As Brutus says to Cassius, the eye cannot perceive itself, it needs "some other thing." Yet, though this claim is mechanistically true, there are vast reservoirs of human reflection—itself a visual metaphor of looking at mirrors—which informs us otherwise. Aristotle tells us in the opening sentences of the *Metaphysics* that we take delight just in seeing—that "all men by nature desire to know." He thus, perhaps unwittingly but far more likely with profound subtlety, initiates his inquiry into what is real by an entirely aesthetic first paragraph. Thomas Aquinas defines the beautiful as that which delights or pleases the senses; Kant, as that which delights or pleases the mind; and Plato, in the *Republic*, assures us that beauty is the only phenomenon that is at once perceived and conceived together, bringing delight by the union of both.

There are two important things to note about this harvest from the extended garden of our philosophical tradition. The first is that the phenomenon of perceived reception seems inevitably to settle, as wanderers or refugees settle, not as sand settles in the bottom of the glass, in the alien land of beauty. The second and far more disturbing is the seemingly unchallenged account of beauty as pleasure, either to the senses, the mind, or both. This suggestion is deeply disturbing since no one seems to want to ask how such a thing as our own mind can have pleasure, for pleasure is surely a sensuous, palpable phenomenon. It seems almost impossible to "please" such things as our minds that have no sensory receptors to receive the pleasure. To say the usage is metaphoric does no good at all, since pleasure is such an immediate and direct phenomenon that metaphoric uses of it require greater adroitness to make it work than is supplied by the metaphor. Even to speak, as Aquinas does, of pleasure to the senses, is somewhat labyrinthian. For the tactile nerve endings on our skin and palate are obvious receptors of pleasing sensations; but it seems entirely asymmetrical to the nerve endings in the ear receiving "pleasure" from a troubling but mighty poem like *The Faerie Queene*. For in this case, it is obviously not the mere excitation of the nerve endings in the ear that is delighted by mere stimulus; as the physical caress on erogenous tissue is the causal agent of the instinctive or automatic pleasure we take just in the touch itself. To say that beauty pleases the senses seems, then, too narrow or too misleading; to say it delights the mind seems usurpatory of palpable sensations by a faculty that has none; and to say it pleases both is therefore to beguile doubly. So there are great dangers in describing, much less defining, beauty as the pleasure given to our various faculties. It is at the very least unsettling, and, hence, must provoke further thought.

Nevertheless, the various claims that perception brings pleasure are persuasive if not compelling. Normally we perceive, especially when we perceive visually, in a practical or utilitarian mode; but sometimes we perceive not as enablements of manipulating our universe but simply for the sake of perceiving. To put it in the vernacular, we seem to *like* to see and to hear and to feel. The most obvious instances of this—though surely not the only ones—are those in which what is perceived has been ripped from its purposive form and isolated from any practical or utilitarian value; some instances of this we designate as art. If the abduction of the phenomenon occurs solely in our approach to it, as when we observe a radiant sunset not as a warning of impending darkness but simply as something to see just for the sake of seeing, we designate this as purely natural beauty, and not art, which always abducts as hostage certain phenomena from their normal occurrences as events, and puts frames or quotation marks around them or places the actions on a stage, thereby exiling them from the homeland of utility.

What attracts us about this account is its simplicity and putative accuracy. Nor do I wish entirely to discredit it, for my quarrel is not with the exile of phenomena from their natural belonging in the realm of praxis, which seems to me accurate enough, though perhaps lacking in depth. Rather, my dispute is with the vagueness and uncertainty of the term *pleasure* as designating the essential response of this banishment from the mainland of utility. It is as if we are compelled to label as beautiful anything that is impractical, which is nonsense. To perceive our own perceiving—which at least in the case of sight seems a grotesque impossibility—cannot be rendered thoughtful simply by appending the psychological, supporting phenomenon that it happens to please us. This adds so little to the explanative account as to be seriously deflated in importance. To say I take pleasure in eating may mean little more than that I do in fact eat without enforcement. To say the reason I attend operas is that they give me pleasure seems vacuously identical to say I go to them; but the deeper question that asks why operas *can* cause pleasure in an audience is profound and illuminating. The term, in other words, when used as a cause or motive adds very little. Further, pleasure is often equated with gratification, reducing its peculiar significance in our understanding of how we can appreciate nobly rather than basely. To argue that the reason we go to art museums is because art brings pleasure may be true, but it contributes such minimal understanding as to be almost worthless, for, barring duress, whatever I do I do in part because to some degree it satisfies. The same answer could be given for why we do *not* go to museums. To say I take pleasure in slaking my thirst—which differs not at all from saying I drink because I am thirsty—is so far removed from wondering why and what it means for me to attend a performance of *Agammemnon* that to account for both by the same psychological phenomenon of pleasure seems to diminish the term entirely as a source of explanation. It is not at all obvious that a sensitive viewer actually takes pleasure in watching *Agammemnon*, especially not if the same term is used to account for scratching one's ear. The term *pleasure* threatens to become a mere formal connector without peer or substitute: whatever I do I do because of pleasure. If this is so, then the term *pleasure* simply means whatever causes me to do something, and that is reduction if not to absurdity at least to impoverishment. If we are to redeem pleasure from the pile of rejected words that have lost their meaning, we must resist these overly facile accounts that render all motivations the same.

Perhaps some redemptive solace can be found in the account of perception as enabling receptivity. Thus, it is the adjective that matters here, not the noun. It is not that I receive that brings pleasure, but that in perceiving I am enabled. Thus, enablement, when directed toward the phenomenon of perceiving itself, is simply what we mean by pleasure in the higher senses of delight taken *solely in the enabling of the perception itself.* Beautiful things enable me to be aware of what it means to perceive, and this new awareness is of a remarkably different kind, in which I am not made aware of items in the environment telling me that something exists but of what it means to perceive at all. There seems to be some truth in the realization that observing a ballet shows us what it means to move, appreciating architecture shows us what it means to dwell, looking at a painting shows us what it means to see, and listening to a sonata tells us what it means to hear. In addition to these general discoveries, since most great artworks have themes and topics, we learn from *Hamlet* what it means to confront the infinite without eclipse, from the *Scarlet Letter* what it means to confront scandal as a foil against integrity, from *Tristan und Isolde* what it means to be in rapture without hope.

This suggests a fourth description of art, following the three views that pleasure is given the senses, that it is given the mind, and that it is given both; namely, that art, as a form of perceived reception, *shows us what it means to be enabled by reception.*

What Does Enabled Reception Mean in Art?

This new definition requires analysis and reflection. We have seen that what it means to perceive is to be able to receive, and that all such reception—that is, all reception that is the result of perception—is existentially meaningful as enablement. In utilitarian and practical cases, which are by far in the majority, such enablement increases control of the environment; but in cases in which the reception itself is enabled, the perception is rendered meaningful independent of its practical usage. To say we learn what it means to dwell through the art of architecture does not mean that the great cathedral keeps us drier and warmer than the peasant's cottage—for indeed the latter may be more comfortable—but that the perceived reception of the architect's artwork enables us to see, perhaps for the first time, or at least newly each time, what it means to dwell. Such discovery is not informational, nor can it be reduced to propositions. Rather, it enables us as receivers to become dwellers. The logic of this suggests that to seek shelter in a peasant's cottage is not to dwell at all, for there is no receptive enablement in our perception of the cottage. This is not to say that dwelling in cottages is impossible, for the introduction of other factors such as familial love, the sacredness of hearth and home, and the rituals of the domicile may provide true dwelling. But these activities are not perceived reception as is the submissive, awestruck wonder at what the cathedral reveals.

The cathedral, like the palace, the mansion, or even the highrise condominium if well decorated, all enable us to submit to the discovery of what dwelling means simply in the perceived reception of the building. However, the cathedral is distinct from the mansion; it may well enable us to dwell, but, more specifically, as a cathedral, it enables us to worship, just as a great opera house like Bayreuth enables us to submit to whatever opera reveals, or a well-designed classroom enables us to learn. The enablement, by the cathedral's architecture, to make worship possible is one of refinement. Druids were able to worship among the forests, and our colonial and puritanical ancestors reviled cathedrals as popish and preferred simple chapels. Nevertheless, the refining, thoughtful architecture of the great cathedrals enables solely on the basis of perceptive reception. If we recognize architecture as an art form, we can then see that the art enables, by the simple acceptance of or submission to the perception, to learn what it means to worship and worshipfully to dwell.

This reinforces the earlier marked observation that perception as receptivity is submissive to the authority of what is perceived; so that I must hear the dreadful thunder whether I want to or not, and, hence, I submit, possibly in fearsome trembling, to its threat of power and violence. In the case of perceiving art, that to which I submit is not a simple event or fact, but the confronted meaning of what is revealed. Like the thunder, I cannot escape it, so there is genuine submission, and accordingly there is the necessary authority inherent in the receptivity to induce submission. But though there is authority, and to some extent, I must submit, as art the very yielding to this authority enables by enriching our understanding of what it means to receive the perceived modality. Concretely, the genius of William Blake compels by its authority my submission to the learning of what it means to confront a tiger:

>Tyger Tyger, burning bright,
>In the forest of the night;
>What immortal hand or eye,
>Could frame thy fearful symmetry?

These lines are not merely accurate, nor are they simply pleasant to hear; rather, they enable through the hearing to confront what it means to share darkly the world with tigers—or to put it more simply: we are enabled to confront what it means for there to be tigers—which is an awesome realization.

To be enabled by the receptivity of and submission to the authority in art takes the form of confronting and learning what it means for there to be whatever is perceived in the artwork. In great art, what we confront and learn may be so complex and varied that identifying what we confront is entirely frustrated. Can we ever identify all of what is confronted in *Hamlet* or *The Ring of the Nibelung*? Such complexity in no way sabotages this description; indeed, it supports it. We are thus enabled by the artwork to accept, even submissively and by force, what it means to confront who we are in the world and what it means to exist in the various ways that the arts reveal.

However, if this is so, we are forced to submit to the angry possibility that not all perceiving is equal; that we do not merely perceive or not perceive, but that we can perceive well or badly, successfully or unsuccessfully. To perceive badly is to fail to receive all that it is possible to receive. This must be the case if we can learn what it means to confront what is offered in the perception of the artwork. Can this be defended or explained? It may seem that all clear-sighted observers of Rembrandt's *Polish Rider* see the painting equally well; that is, their receptive organs and machinery of neural messaging are all functioning properly, and so they all see the painting equally well. They may admit that their interpretive skills differ, but their perceiving does not permit of degrees. If by "perception" we mean the mechanistic procedures by which our sensory organs receive external information and process such reception neurally to the brain, this egalitarian account would be correct. However, we are not asking how our perceptive organs work, but what it means to perceive; and under the rubric of this question degrees of success and failure can and do play an essential role. It seems obvious that we can train the senses. A hunter may practice staring straight ahead but concentrating on the extreme limits of his or her peripheral vision, and through such training increase his or her capacity to perceive movement in the bush. A listener can be trained by a lover of music to attend to various voices at once, thereby hearing the fugue that had not been heard before. The first witnessing of *Richard II* may consist solely of following the complex plot; but discussing the play and revisiting its performance or text may uncover the rich development of the character that makes it so precious to the ages. To deny that these are refinements of perception is to persist in thinking of perception neurologically rather than receptively.

To insist that such refinements are within an entirely separate faculty of interpretation and not perception itself is to argue from a rigidly stipulative definition that, though narrow, admittedly has some support in the history of epistemology. The broader range of the present form of the question that asks what it means to perceive denudes such stubbornness of its concealing drapery. It may take years to develop a palate so judicious as to recognize the special vinegar in a fine sauce; but to deny that the refined taste is a perception defies critical sensitivity. Of course, we can now taste the elusive ingredient after subtle training whereas before we could not taste it; and taste is one of the sensory receptors by which we perceive. For the unsophisticated youth, the failure to taste the vinegar is simply a failure in perception—the perception of taste. To fail to hear the synthesizing counterpoint in Mozart's *Jupiter Symphony* is a failure in hearing—which is a perception. To fail even to see the chiaroscuro in Rembrandt's self-portrait is a failure in seeing, which is a perception. So we can succeed or fail at perceiving, and not merely at some interpretive level of conceptual analysis. I do not conceptually reflect on the taste of vinegar—I only taste it or fail to taste it. The success and the failure is in the perception.

This somewhat involved argumentation is designed to show that if we can succeed or fail as perceivers, then it is by refinement of our own perceiving that we can improve our grasp of what it means to confront the essence of what is perceived. If we can succeed and fail at perceiving, there must be some standard, anchor, or paradigm external to and independent of our private impressions. The relativism inherent in the merely neurological sense of perception, which Plato rejects so vehemently in his reading of Protagoras, places the ultimate seat of judgment in each individual, separate consciousness. Substituting this mechanistic model—which I concede does indeed make each perceiver the measure of all things—with the existential one encrypted in questioning what it means to perceive, relieves the thinker of this skeptical relativism and makes possible the seemingly obvious truth that we can refine our perceptions and, hence, judge them by nonsubjective standards. If the first stage of this quest seems arduous, the effort may nonetheless justify it. If we now can argue that perceptions can be refined by reference to nonsubjective meaning, it is possible to support the claim that such refinement, as a mode of being fine, enables us to confront the essence of what it means to perceive in different ways, and what it means to perceive at all.

Refined Perception

This first mile puts us on a hill allowing for a purview of the unfolding journey. The quest must now travel down a two-stage path of inquiry: first, what does it mean to refine our perceptions; and second and more important, what is meant by essence? The trek thus far has at least yielded its elevation in the foothills of the climb: the fine can be found in perception, and in two ways. First, it is possible to perceive the fine; and second, the perceiving itself can be either fine or crude.

Chapter 2

Perceived Essence

The shift from one chapter to another in the present inquiry is not merely a change of topic, but a further step in the progress of the quest. This advance of the inquiry is marked chiefly by the refinement of the questioning. It was noted in the prior chapter that the poet's fine use of language allows us to focus upon the essence of what we confront. This discovery allows us to ask a more penetrating series of questions.

What Does It Mean to Refine Our Perception?

To refine perception cannot simply mean to perceive extensively, for there are those who reach their seventh or eighth decade having sensed much but learned little and refined not at all. So the mere practice of perceiving something is not the refining of it. It may well be that to rely overly upon the sensory element of perception is actually retrograde to refinement, since the repetitive frequency of certain sensations may well produce mere habit and its consequent bias, shielding us from the very learning that may refine. Nor does the mere openness to new perceptions, found often in the irrepressible curiosity of youth, guarantee refinement, for a wanton hunger for new distractions may be so indiscriminate that the counterill to habit and bias, which is unjudged equality or indifference, may mute the authority in learning. Hence, it is neither the frequency nor the variety of perceptions but the quality of them that leads to refinement. How are we to understand this difference between the refined perception that allows us to learn, and the mere repetitive or newly discovered perceptions that may amplify our knowledge but need not refine at all? The problem is exacerbated by the threat of vague circularity; we must avoid the simplistic maxim that refined perception yields refinement, for though it may be true, it tells us little.

The two terms *learning* and *authority* may, when pressed, reveal something worthy of this problem. To learn is not merely to expand our reservoir of what is known, but to discover truth, especially about one's own existence and its meaning; and consequently, the authority inherent in such learning is the power and persuasion of truth flexed, as a muscle, so as to compel submission to it. For one already educated properly, the truth as truth should be authority enough, but this is to retreat into pleasant but numbing utopianism. Truth may indeed have authority as truth, but the nature of such authority and the willingness to submit to it remain hidden, and any appeal to it is vacuous until it is brought out into the open. Authority unpromulgated is rather like a powerful army kept in its barracks, meaningless unless led onto the battlefield.

We distinguish authority from power; for a tyrant can use brute force to govern reluctant citizens, and even the mere threat of naked brutality in a terrorist regime compels the people to fearsome obedience. This is contrasted with the government of authority, in which the eloquence and wisdom of the leader effectively persuades a people to support even sacrificial policies when they can be convinced of their nobility, as Abraham Lincoln led with magnificent authority the reluctant North to accept emancipation and the continuation of fratricidal war. This distinction is not merely between persuasion and physical duress; it is possible to persuade without authority, as con men do, and legitimate authority at times may also employ coercion, as drill sergeants do. Authority in learning is that which compels acceptance because of truth being flexed, which means truth manifest in such a way as to provoke submission. Not all truth, or course, is flexed; indeed, truth on occasions of great subtlety may be elusive and even shyly reluctant to yield to the inquirer. However, even in such recalcitrant cases, there must be some authority, such as a great teacher who makes us dig energetically to find the buried jewels in the rock. It is in this exercise of nonbrutal authority that the true nature of refinement can be found. Lincoln's noble authority, when examined developmentally, exemplifies this refinement. In his early, frontier eloquence prior to his election, Lincoln taught us first to confront ourselves as we were, denuding the dangers that lurked within and raising the consciousness of the people to confront boldly what other politicians were seeking to obfuscate through jargon and cleverness. He showed us we were a house divided, and could not stand—which is what no one wanted to hear. In his grander, presidential eloquence, his authority was able to achieve a refinement of our learning, in which the nobler and even radiant strains were uncovered, awakening us to the finer heights of self-confrontation. The rare military genius of Lee, which would have split the Union forever except for Lincoln's rarer eloquence, though more intimidating and even more forceful, was in the end not as authoritative. Lincoln's authority over his people lay in his authority in his grasp of the truths inherent in and inherited from his nation; the flexing of the muscle of this truth is his sublime eloquence in the English language and his unflagging trust in the nobility of our inheritance. The address at Gettysburg ennobles—that is, flexes truth—by letting true learning take place. This suggests that the fundamental role of authority is to allow self-learning to occur; and it is precisely the authority inherent in such learning that is refinement.

The prefix seems to suggest that refinement can only be of what is already possessed. Lincoln did not invent the notion of our species of self-government as perhaps Madison may have—though Madison, too, looked back on centuries of speculation and earlier republics. Neither can it be said that Lincoln merely reiterated Jefferson and Madison; in refining he sharpened and honed what was inherited in our tradition, bringing forth overtly what may have been latent or unexpressed, flexing the muscle of the truth hidden within the sleeve of the Constitution and Declaration of Independence. This flexing of the truth refines, not merely because it is more ardent or even more eloquent, but because it is more revelatory of essence. The refinement of the later Lincoln's oratory pierces through the distractions of political everydayness and reveals the essence of the American republic. It is, in many ways, an improvement on the original disclosures, but though it thereby has its own superiority, it is reverential even to the point of near adoration for what occurred four score and seven years before.

So there is a paradox in refinement: it seeks to improve, but reveres as sacred what is already given. Mozart did not invent new forms, he brought them to unparalleled perfection; Shakespeare simply rewrote older and well-known plots, giving them such great authority that they seem entirely new in their power to teach us who we are. Indeed, most great artists are not innovative and creative in the sense of doing what has never been done before—a passion that now unfortunately seems to dominate these fields to the detriment of their offerings—they rather refine and revisit the classic themes and truths, seeking reverentially only to reveal them more profoundly. The person who writes the first sonnet is not remembered, but the one who refines the sonnet to perfection is revered as the greatest poet of our tongue.

This simple observation that the truly great are not the innovators but the refiners is not meant merely to footnote our reading of the history of art—indeed, the insight offered by it reaches far beyond such academic ratings. If great art is always in some fundamental sense a refinement of what is already there, if Lincoln's oratory husbands already seeded patriotic courage that keeps the dismal defeats in Virginia from bringing down the nation, then we have uncovered an extremely significant point about perceptual refinement and the authority inherent in it. If we refine only what is already there, waiting, as it were, to be disclosed or uncovered by the refining artist, then we must see that essence is the true lure of the refiner. Refinement is therefore not decorative but strengthening; it is not adding something new but digging deeply to uncover what is latent, the way Michelangelo seemed to sense the inner figure waiting to be released by his refining chisels.

We can only perceive what is already there; even imagined perceptions are of some recreated representation. If we perceive what already is, and if perception can be refined, then the improved perception is not due to the enhancement of the sensory organs, as spectacles refine our vision, but is rather a tuning of our receptivity better to isolate what is *means* to perceive what is confronted. This isolation or pinpointing of meaning reveals essence. True refinement, therefore, has as its matter the already existing but murky and hidden essence that is to be made radiant. To refine our perception is to submit to the training guided by mastery that permits us to perceive essence by means of learning to confront ourselves. Only when we learn to perceive what is flexed by essence can such self-confrontation take place.

What Does It Mean to Confront Essence?

The concept of essence has long been something of a shibboleth in philosophical analysis, in the sense that it seems available only to the initiates and is deeply suspect of all aliens to a tradition even as it is most precious to those who dwell within it. Essence is contrasted with the trivial; it is what is fundamental in importance; it is what differentiates on the level of what is most real; it is the inner, hidden core, the possession of which guarantees authenticity and the lack of which dooms to endless wonderings. It is the opposite of what is mere shell or surface; it is the ultimate in truth and meaning, the necessary as opposed to the contingent. Yet, for all its glamour, it is elusive in its topography; we ask where it dwells and seem confounded by the question. Is essence within a thing? Is it in a word? A concept? A class? A species? Ludwig Wittgenstein became famous for his critical attacks on verbal essence, showing that terms were more flexible than that, and by escaping from the tyranny of essence one could therapeutically remove oneself from asking meaningless questions. To argue that the locus of essence is the thing itself suggests essence is mere abstraction from similar experiences of those elements that are common, making essence a mere minimalist set of necessary conditions for a concept. In this sense, it is the least that can be said of anything. Descartes's analysis that the essence of corporeal things is extension is a paradigm of such thinking: since all material things must take up space, to say the essence of matter is extension is simply to apply minimalist conditionality for membership in a class. It would seem then, that essence loses its authority if located either in the term or the thing.

If essence is to lie not in the thing itself, nor in our verbal articulation of it in definitions, then where or what is its locus? If Lincoln's oratory penetrates into the essence of the American Republic, we are led to reexamine exactly what this means. What Lincoln shows us is what it means to be an American, not how to define "American" or what political species or kind of thing an American is. Essence is therefore not of terms or entities or even of concepts, but of meanings; and with this discovery a considerable advance is made in the quest: refinement is of essence and essence is the core of meaning. This is not to equate essence with meaning, for the latter is of broader range, the former of deeper penetration. It is to locate essence in the proper realm of discourse so that it now becomes possible to see how essence can be approached through refinement only if it is already meaningful and exposed as that which makes meaning possible. Meaning itself thereby becomes more available to our analysis, permitting at least a provisional suggestion that by "meaning" is meant "that which allows—or provides a ground—

for thinking about something in terms of the possibility of success and failure." This suggestion is provisional only, and should not be analyzed here and now lest it distract; but it does show that the term *meaning* is not some shibboleth in its own right, like some chanted mantra stirring only the elect.

The emerging maxim seems to be that refinement is philosophically significant solely in terms of essence, which in turn is the centrality or synthesizing core of meaning—that is, what makes it possible to think about something in terms of success or failure. If Lincoln's eloquence is a refinement of an already existing truth, the truth in question is not propositional but essential. It concerns itself not with questions of whether—or even of what species—a thing is, which then can be codified into the lawlike forms of propositional predication or class logic, but of how we think of it in terms of its succeeding or failing to be what it is in terms of what makes such thinking possible.

Essence itself, therefore, cannot be thought directly as an object of knowledge or even as a standard by which judgment is assessed. Essence is not what is thought but rather what makes thought possible. It is "making possible" that is the true meaning of authority. Thus, the essence of being American is what makes possible the refining of this through the perceived eloquence—and "authority"—of Lincoln's oratory. We cannot forget that we perceive this address; it is the hearing of it that refines. What then does it mean to hear Lincoln's speech? *It is to submit, through the refining of our hearing, to the authority provided by the essence or truth of what it means to be American.*

There is nothing radical or revolutionary about this, though the care taken with the language may be itself a species of refinement; but to reflect on the elements of this account is entirely worthwhile philosophically. The notion of submission, so essential to our understanding of what it means to perceive, is here joined to the linking notions of authority and meaning in an example that in no way offends, startles, or obfuscates. After all, we ourselves do listen to great speeches, and the Gettysburg Address surely is one; and from this listening, we truly seem to confront what it means to belong to this country's heritage and tradition. What is remarkable is the central role played by refinement in our understanding of this available experience. Since the refining, in this case, takes the form of oratory, it is an aesthetic and, hence, perceived denuding of our heritage: we actually hear what, hitherto muted, it means to be

American. As a perception, such hearing is submissive, and as refined perception, such hearing is submission to the resonance of its essence.

We submit both to power and to authority, but the nature of the submission is radically different in the two cases. Submission to power can neither enlighten nor refine; it is simply cause and effect. The brutal police either actually use their clubs to drive us into enclaves, or so terrorize us by the threat that our own fear drives us to the same destination. Because we are weak we must yield, and in yielding we become even weaker. In submission to authority we are persuasively led rather than pushed into self-recognition, in which our own realization, fruited now with the blossoming of the latent, confronts our essence, denuded or refined of all its concealing artifice, and, hence, demands submission not by force but by attraction. We are thereby strengthened rather than weakened. The crack of the thunder persuades by power—we cannot select not to hear it—but the crack in the walls of our own self-concealment lures us as Carmen lures Don José or Cleopatra lures Antony; our submission is no less compulsive, but in the latter cases, the lure is our own and not alien as is the other.

Yet, there is more to essence than its allure to think about meaning, for there are many ways to think about something, and there are many ways to be meaningful. What it means to be American, as flexed by Lincoln's speech, seems to contain many facets: that we are free, that we live under law, that we are protected from overly intrusive government, that we love our country, and even the simple judgment that we are born here and belong here. Indeed, some of these American qualities seem to conflict in various ways. We seem to believe in a free press, and also to believe in presumed innocence; yet an unrestrained press may well persuade us of the guilt of an untried, unjudged, and ultimately unguilty defendant in violation of his or her right to a just trial. We are loath to restrict the press, but we are also loath to surrender the presumption of innocence. To ask which is more American, to prefer an entirely unbridled press or to protect the reputation of the defendant by curtailing what the press may say, is ridiculous, for we honor both of these institutional guarantees protected by the Constitution. Which is the essence? The right to an unbiased and truly just trial, or the First Amendment's restraint on government not to intrude into a free press? The conflict is real, and each American should be troubled by it; but what is meant by the *essence* of being American is the synthesizing of these vexatious stresses on the grander picture. The essence does not relieve the tension but embraces it, for being American is to dwell in the anguish of precisely these internal struggles that stimulate ceaseless and painful judgment. It is for this reason that essence itself is never isolated and known as an object. The very conflict between a free press and assumed innocence is itself a refining of our submission to the essence of being American. Thus, the essence is an absorbing, synthesizing reality that makes possible not only the conflicts of our antinomic adherence, but also the refinement necessary to join them together. To assume definitive knowledge of essence would destroy what is so compelling: that we yield or submit to it rather than control or define it, reducing it to a mere decision procedure, as if it were a central microchip in the unifying of myriad input.

To yield or to submit—which is the existential basis of perceiving—is not a mark of enslavement or degradation, for only through such submission to the authority of our perception can we learn. Control and submission, usually seen as opposite, can nevertheless be conjoined; for although we must submit in order to receive impressions or to learn from authority as an apprentice learns from a master, we nevertheless also control, as when we refine our perceiving by allowing the essence of what is meaningful to be heard in what we hear or see in what we observe. This refinement can be understood neither as the poet's power to select the perfect, denuding term nor as the listener's attunement to the essence-penetrating authority within the poet's speech, but only by the conjunction of both in the phenomenon of learning. The master craftsman cannot force his authority on an unrefined ear any more than a willing apprentice can learn unless the master offers what is fine. There is no difficulty in this as long as we avoid the folly of assuming only unicausal explanations; indeed, the reduction of this phenomenon of refinement to causes and their effects is entirely misleading if not downright wrong. We do not ask the cause of the fine but the meaning of it.

The confrontation of essence, therefore, cannot be discovered either in the attunement of the listener or the skill of the speaker, but in the broader phenomenon of learning itself. All true learning is self-learning—that is, we learn to become who we are—but such learning is always of ourselves being in the world. We do not learn about the world as an entity other than ourselves, but as the dwelling-place that anchors our belonging to it and in it. The phrase "external world" is therefore a pernicious locution, for it suggests the possibility of a worldless subject coming across an entirely alien object that can in principle be subjectless. But any subject is already in the world, and the world already contains as an essential part of itself the confronting subject. The various ways in which we dwell in the world, such as being American, being a parent, being vulnerable to the authority of experience, are all understood in terms of what it means to be in the world, and each of these various ways of being meaningful have essences that allow these ways to be thought about as meaningful; and these essences are discoverable only through refinement.

To refine is therefore to be in the world in sundry ways, each of which has an essence that forces us to submit to the authority of self-learning. This essence, therefore, cannot be reduced to a series of propositional predicates that constitute the elements that make up a thing, the way bricks and lumber make up a house, but is rather the authoritative power that makes possible our thinking about meaning, the way the authority of a home makes possible our thinking about belonging, exile, welcome, and homesickness. If the essence of a home is that which makes belonging possible, it is the refinement of the home that reveals the authority inherent in this essential meaning. Loving parents, like poets refining language or painters refining the wedding of color and form, refine the welcome of belonging in a myriad of ways, from the kindly but stern discipline of parental authority to the reverence shown the institutional structure, the spontaneous grasp of youthful folly, and the balanced need for comfort and scolding, even down to the well-laid fire, the smell of cooking, the privacy extended to each child, the cheerful listening to the clumsy telling of the schoolboy's misadventures, and the unfathomed trust that assures us we remain welcome even when we go astray. These, too, are refinements, and as fine they show us how to think about what a home means by the hegemony of its essence. To the casual, unfamilied bachelor, these may seem but quaint sentimentalities; but such unrefined perception is a blinkered blindness to the essence that makes possible the perception of what a home truly means.

To confront essence, therefore, is not to isolate some special, minimalist, necessary quality; it is rather, through refinement, to be made able to think about what it means to dwell in the world successfully or unsuccessfully. Essence is never directly perceived the way we perceive the rain; it is learned as that underlying authority that provides meaning. We speak of confronting essence, not perceiving or even knowing it, since our only access to it is through the refinement that sensitizes (i.e., makes possible) our learning of its authority. Thus, although we are already aware of our inevitable death, it is only the fine and penetrating language of Emily Dickinson's poetry that makes possible our learning of what it means to be going to die. What makes such learning possible is called essence, and what makes essence accessible to us is the fineness of her language.

A consequence of this argumentative refinement is this: the act or phenomenon of love has no essence; neither does the term *love* have an essential definition; but what it means to love indeed does have an essence, in part because the refining power of poetic language can evoke a response that the poet's words have pierced through the phenomenon into its essence. Without the refinement, which as fine penetrates, there would be no essence to anchor the judgment that the poet has succeeded in showing us how to think about what love means. It is thus only through the fine that we confront essence.

What Does It Mean to Perceive Without Essence?

The question of perceiving without essence raises the undeniable point that not all perception is fine or even refined and, hence, as coarse does not penetrate to essence. It suggests that to understand the fine, we must also understand the coarse or the unrefined. Since it is obvious that most perception is indeed vulgar in this sense, we must ask what this means. Unrefined perception informs us of what happens in the world; it also provides us with an ever-expanding list of the items that exist within the world. To identify this kind of perception as vulgar is not meant to denigrate it as a source of knowledge nor even to demote it as unworthy of our attention. It is meant to limit it as a resource of meaning, and to some extent, therefore, to see in its predominance a threat to the more refined perception, just as social vulgarity is not only offensive to refined gentility, but actually can erode the authority of the fine. It therefore deserves our attention and analysis.

However, terms such as coarse, crude, or vulgar connote a certain sense of rawness and even uncivilized behavior bordering on the bestial or savage; in some senses, this connotation is exactly what is intended, for few would deny that perceptions that are dulled to that point threaten any penetration to the essential meaning, or even to any meaning whatsoever, as when nonsense is shouted deliberately to intimidate by the assault not only on the ears but on the person. It is not what is shouted but the shouting itself that matters, and when what is shouted is simply meaningless cacophony, the expectation of words having some sense is violated, thereby intensifying the sheer brutality of the howling. This may be the extreme sense of coarseness, and being extreme, it is easy to discredit and reject. There are far more subtle and more dangerous assaults on meaningful perception that are not so blatantly offensive but that must be confronted in order to understand the full range of impediments to penetrating essence.

First Impediment

The first of these perceptive impediments shares none of the qualities of the uncivilized barbarity of the overtly vulgar, but rather impedes any confrontation with, or penetration into, essence by what might be called a fake or deceptive refinement; this is the distortion of our perception through overconcern with the dainty and the decorative known as dandyism, or perhaps even the hypersensitivity of the esthete. This is a more insidious form of vulgarity precisely because it is cloaked in the shallow delicacy that distracts from both meaning and essence by overemphasis on the decorative.

The esthete is not without some contributive significance, for his concerns with the decorative may indeed point out hidden subtleties in the perception that may broaden the thinker's grasp of an expansive work of art. There is often an element of appreciative humor in the esthete's disdain. When the rabble outside the opera house are threatening to bombard the performance as a protest against aristocratic sentiment, carrying placards that read: "Down with the prisy tennors!" the implacable esthete looking down from the balcony may drawl out his contempt by saying they are unworthy of our heed because they are bad spellers, and we appreciate his light-hearted acumen. "They double the n's and singularize the s, my dears; pay this rabble no heed, for surely they are as incompetent in their brawling as in their orthography." We may take delight in the very superiority of such disdain, as we smile at the warm dandyism of Anthony Blanche in Waugh's *Brideshead Revisited* or Sir Henry Wotten in Wilde's *Picture of Dorian Grey*; but such appreciation for their wit cannot eclipse their genuine threat to the integrity of the great and the meaningful. They are indeed suspicious of passion, delighting more in the resplendent gowns of Violetta than in her tragic magnificence echoed in Verdi's music. Anthony Blanche, though charming, is a destructive force in Sebastian's self-corruption, and Sir Henry helps the hapless Dorian to spurn the very conventions of decency that may have saved him from the diabolical erosion of his soul. The estete and the dandy confuse the ornate with the fine; and though they express delicate horror at the label, they are in truth fundamentally vulgar. For if by the fine we mean that which is essence-penetrating, then the opposite of the fine, the vulgar or the coarse, impedes or even entirely overlooks, the essential meaning to anything. The dandy and the estete accomplish this same impediment by adopting the external forms of refinement without the heart and sinew that propels refinement in the first place—the concern with reaching the essence of what is perceived. These delicate vulgarians are like alien spies in our midst and may be far more sinister than the well-armed regiments outside our walls, for they undermine from within, abusing our trust by distracting us to the ornate rather than the truly fine. The estete on the balcony is actually a compatriot of the unruly crowd below, for both undermine the integrity of the profound.

Second Impediment

The second way of distracting from essence may seem less of a threat than an encumbrance. This is perception used, not confronted. It is language in the vernacular, vision as informational, feelings as warnings. In such perception, the utilitarian or beneficial entirely exhausts what is received. When we are told which door leads to the secretary's office, the information fully eclipses all other dimension of perception, for that is all we wanted to know. If the source of the information is a person familiar with the building, we may also feel a faint stirring of gratitude; but if the source is a diagram on the wall, we may—though usually not—sense relief. However, these responses of gratitude or relief are not inherent in the perception itself, but simply are manifestations of our upbringing or the urgency of need. These perceptions are ubiquitous, necessary, and convenient; but they direct our attention away from the perception itself and focus instead on the result. So much of our hearing, seeing, and tactile feeling are like this that their sheer ubiquity seems to deflate any danger or threat. Since we need such enabling information, what on earth could be wrong with it?

There is, in fact, a great deal right with it; but this in no way lessens its threat to the refining of perception. Its very frequency persuades us to the dangerous custom that such is all perception can offer. Therefore, when refinement occurs there is an instinct to look beyond the perception for its explanation. In the practical enablement, perception is not something that permits refinement; all adequately visioned perceivers see such information equally well, and since on rare occasions we do refine our learning, it is extremely difficult to account for this by refinement of perception. We are thus led to the hypothesis that some of us are endowed with a special, peculiar, or even at times unique, interpreting faculty that is entirely distinct from the perception. Why should this be such an awful suggestion? Whether we refine our perception or a special interpretive faculty other than perception, what difference is there between these two suggestions since in either case refinement does indeed occur?

It is of paramount importance that we retain the notion that perception, and not some nonperceptual faculty, can be refined. It is perception, and no other accounting agency, that submits to the authority of what is perceived, and it is only in this embrace of authority that essence can be confronted. If we first perceive equally, and then only in reflective judgment refine ourselves to the authority of what is essential, there is no way to show how a nonreceptive faculty or power can submit. Submission is precisely what perceiving means. The threat of nonessentialist perception is therefore not *that* we perceive in this way, but that the custom of thinking about perception solely in this way produces the need to invent an entirely separate function of our consciousness that collapses into insignificance because all such a function or faculty could do is to pinpoint the fact that we can refine without showing how such refinement is possible. It is possible because meanings (alone) have essences, and the attunement of our perception to such essential meaning is all we need. We are thus saved from the infinite regress of multiplying endless faculties to account for distinction of kind rather than degree.

Third Impediment

The elaborate (though not refined) language of the esthete and the vernacular, informational language of the guidebook are threats to refinement by distraction; they impede our understanding of what it means to refine. Hence, their danger must be embraced because they both offer other benefits and can be tranquilized by keeping them within the confines of their proper location. The third danger is aggressively offensive, seeking not some proper vessel that may overflow, but like an attacking army, seeking actual destruction of any refinement whatsoever, and consequently seeking also to annihilate the essence itself. This is the harsh, deliberately vulgar coarsening of perception, which in its assault, self-consciously identifies refinement as an enemy to its cause. Hence, it is not the innocent vulgarity of the uninformed or uneducated, for this provokes a sadness or pathos that would seek to educate rather than to sequester the offender. Rather, the truly vulgar perceiving manifests a deep antipathy to both refinement and essence.

Stated this way as an abstract principle, it is easy enough to accept in general terms but does nothing to throw light on what it means to perceive coarsely. The problem is to spot the nature of this coarseness properly, for indeed coarseness itself can in the hands of art enhance our perception and refine it. Even those musicians noted for their refined sweetness, such as Mozart, Schubert, and Puccini, on occasion can use dissonance or even harsh cacophony to vitalize the dramatic content; the finest dramatists often use harsh and vulgar language to reinforce their scenes; great painters such as Goya do not shy away from grotesque depictions of suffering. How, then, do we distinguish these legitimate uses of the coarse from those that coarsen the perception itself? We do not see these examples as mere exceptions to the rule, nor do we even account for them by appealing to their contrast, as if the harsh scene, passage, or visual depiction of anguish serve merely to reinforce the fine by comparison with the rude and vulgar. Rather, we rightly see them as essential for the art form. This would seem to make the coarse a mere subset of the fine and, hence, not a form of perception that threatens the fine.

Yet, the distinction remains licit and essential. The tactile sensations provide us with a curious but profoundly revealing paradox that, if properly viewed, can help us to see the underlying significance in a more subtle and finer way. Two young lovers discover an enchanting, isolated, arcadian spot on the beach. They strip for a swim; he returns to their outspread blanket on the sand, and while she continues to play in the gentle foam of the sea, he lies face down to wait in the soothing rays of the sun. He feels a wondrous touch, intimate, delightful, and arousing. But when he turns, he discovers to his horror that the caresses have come from a lecherous middle-aged man taking advantage of his vulnerability. The original feelings of intimacy and delight turn instantly to revulsion and disgust. Yet, the touch itself was as delightful and provoking as hers would have been. How are we to make sense of this?

What bothers the youth to the point of profound disgust may well be that he enjoyed it in his ignorance, that his arousal, depending on his false assumption it was his beloved, seems now a defilement and a corruption. But if the caress itself pleasured him, why does he reject it as a grotesque violation, one for which the memory now causes acute embarrassment? The pleasing touch is exactly the same whether the vile molester did it or the wondrous girl of his passion did it. It is the essence that matters; the essence of her touch was made possible by their love; the cause—hence, not the essence—of his was made possible by usurpatory lust. Her touch, the essence of which is love, can refine his sensitivity to their mutually shared carnality; his touch, the cause of which is a form of rapine, coarsens what it means to yield to the carnal. Coarsened carnality repudiates the essence of intimacy, and there can be no doubt that this is exactly what the young man feels: an abuse or defilement of what ought to be wonderful. Yet, it is still the touch that defiles and the touch that refines; it is not how he thinks about the two instances of caressing but the pleasured submission to the perceived touch that causes both disgust and delight. The youth's distress is not that he was touched by the defiler but that he took perceived pleasure in it. Such violative touching abuses the essence of carnal intimacy, which is why we can refer to it only in causal and not essentialist terms. If the youth is rather sensitive, he may be unable to take delight even in her touching for some time until he can forget not how he thought but how he felt.

It is therefore possible to defile the perception itself, and such defilement consists in disjoining the perception from what it is supposed to mean—its essence. Vulgar language is not merely coarse, for artists may use coarse language effectively and even beautifully, but it is language that makes our own being able to hear unendurable or repulsive. A play that consists entirely of coarse characters speaking coarse language is vulgar because it makes the act of hearing something to which we cannot submit, but rather something that, in hearing it without its essence being manifested, is merely endured. The rejection of our own hearing, if repeated enough, can close off all access to the essence of hearing, which is submission to the authority of articulated meaning. Vulgar language, unredeemed by the power of art to turn it into a powerful authority, renders our hearing so coarsened that there is no authority at all, but simply brute force and the subsequent rejection of it as meaningful.

The example of the sexually usurped youth on the sand may be misleading. The point is not moral: the young man's lover could also be male and the usurper a syphilitic whore trying to persuade him to go straight; or the young lovers could be married and the usurper a jealous enemy. It is not the ethics of it, but the meaning of it that matters. Even on this level, there is danger of misreading. At first it may seem that the entire story repudiates the presupposition of this section, for the argument may proceed along these lines: since both the usurping violator and the loving girlfriend or wife produce equal pleasure on the purely perceptual level—that is, on the level of nerve endings being excited and aroused by touching—it follows that perception is the same in both cases, and that the subsequent disgust with the one and joyous love with the other must be due to some mode or faculty other than perception. If one views perception merely as the provocation of nerve endings and their neural messaging to the brain, this account would be correct and the entire focus of our first chapter would be seriously, if not fatally, undermined. Under such narrowly defined accounts of perception, there can be no refinement whatsoever. However, the argument here is that perception is not the mere neurological phenomenon so described, but is rather the part of our meaning that submits to authority. We do not ask for the mechanics of perception but what it means to perceive. Only in this existential-ontological formulation is perception capable of success or failure, and only so is it possible for perception to be a penetration to essence. It is in this sense that the example succeeds, for we admit that on the neural-messaging level both touches are the same, but in the meaning of being touched, only the refined can penetrate to the essence of submitting to the wondrous authority of carnal love, whereas the usurper's touch can only be accounted for by causes.

Whether the perception be tactile, visual, or oral, the key element is that such perceptions admit of degree, that we can perceive well or badly, and that to perceive well is to penetrate toward the essence—though perhaps never completely to achieve it; whereas to perceive badly is either to impede or even in the more grotesque forms to attack and destroy the essence that makes such perceptions of meaning possible.

It may be helpful to approach the argument from the other end. Using the same example of the boy on the beach, we begin in the classical style of presentation: (1) Essence is defined as that which makes meaning possible; (2) the essence revealed by perception is that which provides the authority of meaning to which the perceiver submits; (3) the essence of the carnal caress is the erotic love that brings together the toucher and the touched in an authoritative union to which both submit in joyous receptivity; (4) when she touches him the submission is guided by the authority of the essence of the erotic love; (5) when the usurper touches him his reception of the touch brings pleasure; but (6) when he sees the usurper, the boy is forced—not led by authority—to experience the powerful perception known as revulsion; (7) this revulsion and its ensuing disgust are legitimate, authoritative feelings that are grounded in the essence of being intimately abused, but they function as manifestations of the blocking of the essence of erotic love. (8) Thus, the revulsion, which is itself a powerful perception, serves as a painful resource of what has been violated: the refinement of the carnal perceptions to penetrate to the essence of true erotic loving.

The example is of the intimate perception of erotic touching, but the principle ranges over the entire landscape of all perceptions, including emotional feelings. Vulgar language abuses the authority of speech by replacing it with the sheer power of an intimidating cause; obscene sights abuse the authority of vision by replacing it with forced recognition of the repulsive, which causes us to turn our face away from it. Forceful causes are therefore antithetic to authoritative essence; the latter allows learning to occur, the former forces mere endurance or resentment.

In the earlier part of this chapter, mention was made of a metaphoric depiction of "truth flexed" like a muscle. The example of the erotic abuse is a form of this flexing, which now can be concretized more finely. It is for this reason that the argument insists that the locus of refinement be perception. These are not abstract, propositional reflections, removed from immediacy by conceptual distancing. Both the repulsion and the joy of the carnal touch are not sterilized by the plastic wrapping of disembodied propositions, neatly catalogued in the vast repository of the museum of possibilities. They are felt—hence, as feelings, are perceived. We can learn what it means to feel only when our perceptions are refined by the authority provided by that which makes meaning possible, the essence, and when this authority is submitted to by the refined perception. To flex the muscle of truth is thus to refine our sensibilities to the point at which we can learn the essential meaning.

The sensibility that submits to the authority of essence is fine. It is not merely refined, which is a learning to submit, but is actually fine itself.

Chapter 3

The Aesthetics of the Fine

> Give me my Romeo; and when he shall die,
> Take him and cut him out in little stars,
> And he will make the face of heaven so fine
> That all the world will be in love with night,
> And pay no worship to the garish sun.
>
> —*Romeo and Juliet*

Why Juliet selects the word "fine" to describe what Romeo's image would do to the night sky reveals much about what might be called the aesthetics of the fine. To grasp this in its dramatic meaning requires some careful probing into the text.

The third act of the play *Romeo and Juliet* is pivotal, and the central images of light and dark are here reversed from the preceding passages. When Romeo first sees Juliet, he spontaneously and instinctively expresses the suddenness of his delight: "She doth teach the torches to burn bright!" Later, in the balcony scene, her appearance is also greeted in radiant terms—"It is the east, and Juliet is the sun!" He even contrasts the sun with the pale moon envious of its brightness, and so the central image that reflects their love is light; a seemingly fitting and proper metaphor for the youthful adolescents ensnared in the most confusing of all human passions. As Juliet awaits the promised arrival in the night of her beloved, the terrible pendulum swings, and the central images dominating the rest of the play are night and darkness. Their enemy is daylight and all that goes with it: exposure, practicality, even perhaps a kind of reality. With this they contrast the lover's deeper reality of night, in which the amorous rites are performed in secret, under the cover of black night's protection. This inimical counter to the lover's preference for darkness is described as "garish"—the counterimage of the fine. What is garish is lacking in refinement; it is overly illuminated, like neon on a busy avenue, harsh in its brilliance, offending the eyes with too much glare. After their lovemaking, the pair quarrel over which bird sings, the nightingale or the lark, the herald of the morn. It is only when Romeo expresses his willingness to die for her self-deceit that Juliet awakens to the true garishness of daylight: risking the death of Romeo. So night and darkness are dear, day and light alien. That the form of tragedy itself is often described as going from light to dark, in opposition to comedy, which goes from dark to light, cannot here be forgotten. It is only in the tomb scene that darkness takes on again its usual gruesome character of death, when Juliet, awakened, looks around her shady surroundings and laments the lack of light. Prior to that the lovers seek out darkness as their friend.

Still, the contrasts between light and dark are not simplistic. In the citation above, it is admittedly the night sky that will be starred with Romeo's figure; but the starry figure itself is a source of radiance and nobility that will move the world to prefer night to day. The darkness favored by the lovers is not that of bleakness or blindness, but of gentle privacy, sheltering us from the raucous; a subdued, muted illumination, more starlit than absolutely black. Romeo's figure in the night sky makes it "fine" as opposed to "garish," suggesting gentility of all the senses: soft-spoken rather than loud, smooth rather than rough, sweet rather than sour. There is more than mere gentility in this fineness; there is also a species of nobility inherent in it that gives the metaphor special significance. This nobility, as opposed to the garishness of open day, guides the lovers in their nightly endeavors and, hence, becomes night's beacon, so that the ennobled darkness can now be seen. To be fine as opposed to garish here means we are not blinded by the harsh sun but led by the sparkle of the stars, the way noble leaders persuade their people to sacrifice rather than the way tyrants compel their people to savagery through fear. The noble guides by uplifting us from the garishness of the daily to the rarity of the fine, in which the double entendre of "daily" is read both as "common" and as "in daylight."

This distinction between the fine and the garish is not restricted to Juliet's fierce and powerful speech in the beginning of act 3. (Juliet by the way, is a stronger character than Romeo throughout the entire play.) Rather, the distinction runs through the entire drama as a leitmotif and is revealed in a complex, dialectical form that shows not only the difference between the fine and the garish but also their interdependence. This interweaving of the two seemingly opposing types, a garish love and a fine love, is absolutely critical to the artwork as a whole, and since it is dramatically resonant of the theme of this quest, deserves some probing.

In each of the two households, there are characters that represent the garish or coarse views of love. Among the Montagues, the chief representative of this is Mercutio and his hotheaded and hot-tongued colleagues; among the Capulets it is the nurse. The nurse and Mercutio are soul mates, much closer to each other than to their own houses. They look upon love as a merry sport, evoking from the nurse a bawdy laughter and from the shrewd Mercutio a bawdy contempt. For both, the physical pleasures of love are the most important. Indeed, our first meeting of the nurse shows her peasantlike delight in the bawdy references to the infant Juliet made by her departed husband who promises Juliet's future delight will not be her infantile lying on her tummy but on her back. This nanny of fair Juliet is a warm, friendly, well-meaning but unrefined character who quickly charms the audience with her irrepressible enthusiasm for life's simpler pleasures. She has also charmed Juliet, for it is obvious that the girl catches the contagion of this robust spirit, as she giggles at the suggestion of her approaching and fresh carnality, producing an infectious delight in her eagerness for uncomplicated and direct joy. Indeed, the nurse becomes a coconspirator with Juliet in her attempt to woo Romeo, so that in this first blush of passion Juliet finds in her a trusted and reliable friend, perhaps dearer to her even than her mother.

Mercutio is less charming but far more intelligent; his wit is more biting than bawdy, though his views on love are earthy enough. Like Juliet's fondness for the nurse, Romeo is at first fond of his scabrous friend; and indeed the young lover's attraction for the absent Rosalind seems more a longing for her sexual favors than for her. In the first act then, both Romeo and Juliet are entirely in agreement with their bawdy friends, Mercutio and the nurse. Indeed, there is no reason why this should not be so, for the carnal is a wondrous and powerful force, especially for these teenagers of such spirited character. We the audience find both Mercutio and the nurse entirely attractive and obvious friends to the young lovers. Unlike the nurse, however, Mercutio does not favor the match, possibly because the special friendship with Romeo may take second place if Romeo successfully woos Juliet but more likely because his contempt for the common includes the commoner elements of bawdy lovemaking. Their original presence is undoubtedly one of support for the title pair, even if their views on love are "garish."

These attitudes of Mercutio and the nurse, even as they are shared in the early acts of the play by Romeo and Juliet would not be of much significance were it not for the sudden and dreadful realization on the lovers' part that such feelings are entirely alien to their newly discovered depths. Romeo must disassociate himself from the wranglings of Mercutio and his friends, not merely because he now is united with their enemy, the Capulets, but because Mercutio's contempt is precisely directed at the very profundity of love that Romeo, a mere dozen hours before, had scarce realized was possible. "He jests at scars that never felt a wound," is not merely an angry retort at Mercutio's teasing, but an aching realization that he and Mercutio now cannot share what matters most to Romeo—a new, terrifying, but splendid kind of love fully at odds with the carping of Mercutio's contempt. Romeo has passed over a bridge of no return, one that the fiery Mercutio can never cross.

It is Juliet's rejection of the nurse that is by far the more spectacular dramatic event. In her anguish, the love-stricken girl suddenly discovers that the nurse simply cannot grasp the nobility of her love for Romeo, since she urges her to yield the vows to the young Montague and placate her father's ire by marrying poor Paris. Juliet finds she must dismiss her onetime friend entirely, for since the nurse cannot grasp the nobility of it, she no longer can be Juliet's true confidante. It was perhaps naive of Juliet to expect the nurse to comprehend these depths, but once the young Capulet realizes this, she feels utterly abandoned, with no close, female friend anywhere to help her. It is not so much that she loses the nurse as that the nurse has, in a profound sense, abandoned her. Accordingly, Juliet is required not merely to mistrust the nurse, but to cut her off entirely. It is a savage learning in which the girl becomes the woman, but it is doubly hard since this was the one woman with whom she has shared everything and who alone should have known the uncommon nature of her belonging to Romeo.

The nurse should have known, Juliet believes. Mercutio should have known, Romeo believes. The abandonment of trust in their recent friends is deep and painful; but they both realize it is inevitable. The way the nurse and Mercutio understand love is simply garish and, hence, must be rejected by those who now have reached the fine.

But here is the paradox. The bawdy, garish love that must be antipodal to the fine is necessary for the fine to emerge. The fine is not some abstract, spiritual, dispassionate appreciation of the beloved, as nuns and monks might love their God. Indeed, the fine love of Juliet for Romeo, and to a slightly lesser degree of Romeo for Juliet, is profoundly erotic, deeply carnal. We the audience need both the nurse and Mercutio to make palatable to us the earthy origin of this grandly fated love. But how are we to understand this? Is it merely contrast? That is, do we note the superiority of the later love over the earlier garish love because of the contrast between the base and the noble? The terrific character of the nurse and the admirable superiority of Mercutio cannot merely be seen as lower forms to enhance by contrast the greater. Mercutio helps us understand who Romeo is; and the nurse shows us the earthiness of Juliet. Yet, in spite of these origins, the garish lights of Mercutio and the nurse must give way to the fine nobility of a love that prefers night's sacrificial and even sacramental death to the base commonness of day and life.

The fine, therefore, is not the mere opposite of the garish, but a species of what might be called "embraced surpassing," in which the base origins are sadly replaced by the mature isolation necessary for full development. It is thus not rejection but necessary surpassing that marks the lovers' taking leave of their former trusts. Juliet's break from the nurse is more sudden and, hence, more shocking, and it comes at a time of dire need for solace; Romeo's isolation is presaged by his fey sense of being fate's child, and is followed by the need to avenge Mercutio's death. In both cases, the audience cannot help but note that what separates them forever from the more common origins of their love is the rarity of their newly discovered passion; it brings them to a land unpeopled by the likes of the nurse and Mercutio, perhaps even by the likes of most people, who being most are common.

What is the real nature—or essence—of this difference? Surely it is not merely a matter of intensity of feeling, for that is transient. The citation begins "when Romeo dies" suggesting the measure of their love is death, not life. When Romeo, knowing full well it is the lark, agrees to Juliet's deceit that it is the nightingale, he admits he "has more will to stay than care to go," and freely embraces the death offered by daylight simply because "Juliet wills it so." Even in his last moments, he wonders if death itself be amorous. There seems, then, to be in the fine love of Romeo and Juliet an intimacy and even willingness to death itself, which so contrasts with the life-centeredness of the garish love enjoyed by the nurse and abused by the wit of Mercutio. These young people are not morbidly distracted by death as a fetish; they love life as much if not more than the garish do. But the fine is not only a quality, it is a perspective; it places things in the prismed light of the transient and the eternal. That is what makes it truly fine.

It is only after his death that Romeo, by Juliet's prayer, becomes eternally fine in the vault of heaven; the garish lasts as long as life, the fine partakes of the infinite. It is an essential quality of the fine that it be set within the many faces of a single diamond, glittering with all the beams and shadows of the constant and the changing, the eternal and the transient, the living and the dead.

With this reminder from the youthful love tragedy, we can turn again to one of the first questions raised by consideration of the mature tragedy that began the introduction. Cleopatra's magnificent lament on the corpse of Antony provokes the unpleasant suggestion that the fine is often recognized only in its loss. We see now that this is not merely a dramatist's technique for evoking a tragic response in the audience. For finite, living beings, the only way to be distracted from the blinding light of garish day is to do violence to it; and that violence is never as effective or as universal as death revealed aesthetically, distanced by art. The garish light of common day blinds us in two ways: it lets us see life only as the fleeting present; and it keeps us from apprehending the whole orb of the world, by eclipsing its second half, night. To see life disjoined from death is not to see life at all but to be blinded by its brightness. Cleopatra, who discovers the true worth of Antony only in his death is actually more magnificently self-deceived than Juliet, who constantly sees death and its metaphoric companion, night, as the wisdom that makes their love fine rather than garish.

This suggests that the fine embraces finitude, the garish disregards it. Let us gather our joys while we may, achieving not a confrontation with but a disregard of death. When Romeo, knowing full well that dawn intrudes, offers to sacrifice his life simply because of Juliet's will, we transcend the mere distractive appeal of a carnal carpe diem and face death as a necessary ingredient for sacrifice, without which there would be no possibility of a fine or noble love. From the intense carnal desire he has for Juliet, which all boys share as a stunning awakening of their manhood, to the overwhelming realization that he would gladly die for her, which as embraced lifts his loving from hedonistic to sacred principles, Romeo becomes a guiding, polar star in the face of heaven. Death is now rendered precious, for through it alone can Romeo reify his sacred, sacrificial offering to his Juliet. To disregard death, as the garish, earthy lovers like the nurse must do, forfeits the possibility of its sacredness and its fineness. A world bereft of possible sacrifice is garish; one in which death and suffering make sacrifice possible is fine. So the noble and radiant meanings of the fine are now wedded to the etymological meaning of finitude and mortality, not as a species of nihilism, but as a bestowal of the sacred through sacrifice.

To some extent, therefore, what brings to the fine a sense of the noble is its sacrificial offering; but on a deeper level, which only the fine can achieve, this nobility is seen as a reverence for truth. The garish, in its blinding glare, deceives; the fine, in the muted velvet of the night, reveals. The young lovers accept their mortality as an essential part of their passion rather than, like garish lovers do, seek to avoid it by gleeful distraction. Yet, fine love is but a refinement of common love, in which the refinement consists of intensifying what it means to love as mortal and as finite and, hence, as a disclosure of truth confronted rather than truth avoided. Each of the three elements in this account is of crucial importance: (1) the refinement is always of meaning; (2) death and finitude are always confronted in the fine, in part because the sheer excellence of the fine is worthy of outlasting our fleeting life spans; and (3) the fine as essence-penetrating is the fundamental manner of confronting truth. The second of these elements—that the fine always mirrors our mortality—accounts for the tragic truth that loss, or the fear of it, seems necessary for the fine, so that *art immortalizes mortality*, as Keats's comments on the Grecian urn so artfully reveal. The fine cuts the finite into stars in the face of death and achieves a kind of infinity.

What is the venue of these brief reflections on Shakespeare's play? These insights seek to illuminate a simple passage by Juliet in which the fineness of Romeo's love contrasts with the garishness of common love, but a mere reading of a single passage does not constitute an aesthetics. Does this reading claim that all true aesthetical judgments, rather than pleasing the observer in some way, consist of making judgments of the fine as opposed to the vulgar? Or does it claim that only some artworks are fine, or even that only some parts of some artworks are fine? Perhaps it is even less: perhaps the analysis merely applies to this single play? Is the love of Romeo and Juliet fine, or is Shakespeare's artistry fine? Or do the variety of these possible questions rest on faulty disjuncts entirely, so that in some sense all of these are meant, even though taken singly they may seem to contradict?

Juliet contrasts the fineness of Romeo with the garish. This can be found in the text of the play. Upon reflection, we learn that it is not merely Romeo the youth who is fine, but their love is as well, in contrast to the garish love mirrored in the attitudes of Mercutio and the nurse. However, in realizing this, we sense not a particular fact but a universal judgment: it is finer to love nobly than garishly. This is not a mere ethical lesson or even a how-to prescription for success in lovemaking; it suggests a refinement of our perception: we *see* now, through the refining of our senses by Shakespeare's fine language, the elegance and superiority of a fine love over a vulgar one. If we refine our perception, we are dealing with aesthetics in the etymological sense; and so we say not only that Romeo is fine and that his love of Juliet is *re*fined by his sacrificial self-realization, but also that Shakespeare's fine language makes available to us the truth concerning what the fine means. Thus, although perhaps not all art need be fine, the understanding of what all artworks mean can best be judged by the fineness through which they reveal what their themes or perceptions mean. We identify such judgment as either fine (i.e., penetrating toward the essence) or crass (i.e., dulling the penetrative power). No artwork can be entirely crass, but *Titus Andronicus* is less fine than *Romeo and Juliet*. So perhaps there are false dichotomies in the original list of questions.

To speak of "the aesthetics of the fine" permits a strong or a weak reading. The latter simply claims there are certain artworks that can be made coherent by understanding how they refine our perceptions so that the meaning of what we perceive is made available. The former claims that all artworks are in fact refinements of our perceptions so as to allow meaning to be brought forth, and that as a consequence there is a standard or a set of criteria by which any and all artworks can be judged: namely, how well the artwork succeeds in revealing through refinement what it means to submit to the authority of the perception. The weak reading seems fairly noncontroversial, for to deny it would disallow any role that refinement might play in any artwork. The stronger claim, however, in its boldness seems too sweeping. There are apparently artworks that do not refine at all, but achieve their effectiveness by cold, harsh denudings that seem entirely retrograde to the delicate, the gentle, or the refined.

Nevertheless, it is the stronger or bolder claim that deserves our attention. It is not obvious that the harsh denuding of some very effective artworks cannot itself be seen as a kind of refinement. The fine should not be equated with mere delicacy or attention to subtle detail. Fine gold means pure gold, unalloyed with the base; and very often such refining, as in the case of refining metals, requires the fierce purging of intense fire to burn away the cruder ore. We have noted that, in the reading of *Romeo and Juliet*, fine love is common love refined; we cannot entirely disjoin the bawdy love from the loftier, a truth recognized by Socrates in Plato's *Phaedrus*. There is no reason to corral so narrowly the method or technique of refinement; toughness can also refine.

The Tough

This concept of toughness deserves a special heading; first, to make sure that the notions of refinement and subtlety are not misconceived as the merely delicate or even dainty, and second to allow a further deepening of what is meant by the aesthetically fine. We speak of physical exercise as strengthening or toughening the muscles, toning them to the level of excellence. We also speak of moral and spiritual toughness, as in the development of courage and loyalty, which endows us with the resilience or endurance to withstand assaults against our integrity or our belonging. With these metaphors we are assisted in seeing the tough as a dimension of the fine. Perhaps they suggest even more: that the tough is part of the very nature or essence of the fine. This cannot or at least should not be left as a mere suggestion; it requires tougher refinement.

The appealing but original metaphor of toughening muscles to refine the body may be more fertile than its simple imagery offers. Exercise can be justified for at least three reasons: it improves our health; it improves our looks; it is enjoyable in itself. All three may overlap in a single exerciser, but the differences deserve reflection. The Greek justification seems nobler than the rest: exercise produces a beautiful body; the modern justification is more pragmatic and even beneficial: exercise improves health. The hedonistic justification seems necessarily subjective: some love to exercise, others hate it. It is the second or health-producing image that should begin this analysis, since part of the reason we enjoy the beauty of well-toned bodies is their radiance of apparent health, especially as youthful health; and part of the reason some enjoy exercise is the feeling of being healthy or youthful. In any event, the justification of exercise by an appeal to health is the most available for analysis.

This raises a troubling question. How do we think of health? Is health natural and disease an external intrusion, almost unnatural? Or is health achieved, as a resistance to natural decay, inevitable aging, and death? Is the newborn infant, with all organs fresh and untried, the paradigm of health; or is the trained, beleaguered, scar-toughened, and disease-immunized fighter a truer representative? The question is neither as casual nor as trivial as it may first seem, for what we mean by health may alter the entire significance of the metaphor. If health is essentially tough—that is, achieved not only through training but also through the endurance of diseased assault rather than the mere natural glow of untried, unsullied youth—then the entire traffic of our ideas about it is guided by a different set of signals, rights of way, and maps. If the ragged tree on the tor, savaged by storms that trim the weaker limbs is healthier than the lush, unruffled greenhouse tree, the metaphor of health is not that of natural purity but of toughened maturity. The endurance and the painful training or exercise is then a form of refinement toward a health achieved rather than a natural health bestowed by nature. From the moment of birth, the infant is on its way to death, as sinews stiffen and the protection of baby fat recedes making falls more painful. Disease begins at birth, slowly draining the vital force from the natural bloom of innocent, raw animality. It is only the toughened who can endure these assaults just because the refinement of toughness makes endurance possible.

The tough suggests the resilient as well as the steady; one who, if knocked down simply rebounds, sloughing off the minor defeat of the battle for the sake of the major confrontation of the war; or the person who, in the midst of myriad distractions keeps an eye on what matters, unfettered by the trivial. It is the tough focus on the important that corresponds to the essence-penetrating quality of refinement. The tough resists the allure of the irrelevant and thereby frees the essential meaning to become manifest. There are tough poets, like Ezra Pound, "This South Stinks of Peace!" and tough dramatists like Tennessee Williams, and tough novelists like

Fyodor Dostoyevski. Their toughness consists of bold and direct denuding of those secret weaknesses we would keep hidden except when genius rips away the concealing by means of refined strength.

Tough art is not always a depiction of harsh things; for one can toughly reveal the tenderness of a gentle love, as Shakespeare often does in his comedies. Is not the rude shepherd Silvius in *As You Like It* rather harshly dealt with by the coarse rejections of Phebe? Yet his is the purest love in the forest. In the case of the same poet's "slave sonnets," we see an almost grisly denuding of erotic enslavement that touches so deeply we almost wish the poet had not exposed his secret so blatantly. Cornwall's harsh "Out! vile jelly!" when plucking out the hapless Gloucester's second eye is harsh and vulgar, to be sure; but to blind a man with passages of Oberonlike sweetness and magic would belittle and even insult the truth. Yet in these examples, we can find powerful penetrations into the essence of refinement. In the aesthetic sense, refinement means penetration to the essence, and toughness can do this.

However, not all senses of the tough are refined. Just as the esthete is distinguished from the fine in the previous chapter, so toughness must be made distinct from the crude. There is a lamentable current in the present tide of art criticism that ranks shock as the supreme achievement. The ghoulish display of human viscera trembling in pain and trauma may stun us with revulsion, but this manipulation of our basest sentiments is cheap and ultimately tiring. It is not truly tough, for it does not reveal meaning; it is rather a morbid fascination with the titillation of shock value for its own sake, and is thus ultimately boring. Repeated scenes of explicit sexual seaminess do not toughen or even really shock, but simply coarsen. The sordid has no special claim upon reality. Why should nihilistic vulgarity be any more real than the struggle for nobility? Pollyanna may be vulgar, too, achieving the same as the sordid: a revulsion unredeemed by truth. Nothing is more transient than the cheap thrill of simple shock; its aftertaste is self-disgust and ultimate indifference. There is nothing tough about it at all.

Aesthetic toughness as a form of refinement penetrates to the essence, understood as that which makes meaning possible; but the tough does this in a way that overcomes reluctance and thereby strengthens our perceptions. We learn harsh truths by way of toughened, nonfrivolous refinement of what it means to perceive things that, in their presentation, astonish, shock, astound, and even scar. The theme itself may be severe, as when Antony rails in outrage over the body of Caesar; or it may be something neutral but presented boldly. Vincent van Gogh paints a bowl of yellow sunflowers, a seemingly pleasant and innocent theme, but the sensitive tough viewer sees (and feels) anger, boldness, even daring in his presentation. There is a toughness here that is felt; it is perceived independent of what we may know of his biography and personal torment. The tough is accordingly not the same as the coarse. If the metaphoric comparison with health has any validity, we see that toughening our perception allows the essence to be perceived the way denuding reveals the naked or fire purges away impurity, in which the pure and the naked are seen as achieved entrances to otherwise protected secrets. That the tough can force its way into sacred precincts is itself a refinement of our own satisfaction with the noble and the bold. The tough refines.

The academic sense of the term *aesthetics* means the way or ways in which artworks and even naturally beautiful objects can be thought about. To say there is an aesthetics of the fine is thus to say that artworks and natural beauty are intelligible by reference to the refinement of our perceptions, which, as fine, penetrate into the essence of what it means to submit to the authority inherent in perception. The perception of natural beauty, therefore, would have to depend on the refinement of our perceptual learning, so that simple, untutored delight in seeing natural things either would not be accounted for, or would be seen as dependent upon the refinement bestowed by art. It is possible to ease this seeming demotion of natural beauty by maintaining that the aesthetics of art is simply quite distinct from the aesthetics of nature. One might even argue that natural beauty is to be seen as a kind of divine artwork. For the sake of this quest, however, it suffices to show that the fine can be seen as the ultimate basis of explanation for how we think about artworks. The purpose of this chapter is not to develop an actual aesthetics of the fine—which would be a book-length endeavor—but simply to enrich our understanding of what it means to say there can be fine perceptions, or that perceptions can be refined. Art is usually seen as perception disjoined from practicality, or somehow separated from our everydayness by "aesthetic distance." As a consequence, it seems to allow for a privileged access to perception as perception rather than perception as a mere element in practical activity or in knowledge. In this sense, the fine perceived is reflected in perception refined.

Chapter 4

Becoming Fine

In *fin de siecle* London, two English gentlemen make a wager. A professor of phonetics arrogantly proclaims that within six months he can train a guttersnipe flower girl to speak such fine English that she can be paraded before royalty and deemed a lady. Colonel Pickering, a wealthy scion recently returned from British India, promises to pay for all the costs should the experiment succeed. Professor Henry Higgins takes the cockney flower girl, Eliza Doolittle, home, and with delightful chauvinism and irresistible snobbery drills her rigorously with phonetic excellence until, at a royal ball, the former flower girl dazzles even the visiting queen, thereby winning for Higgins the wager he had made with Pickering. Eliza's refinement in her speech, however, has wrought a deeper transformation; she has actually refined herself and become a true lady. This presents some warm and delightful developments in George Bernard Shaw's 1912 comic *bildungsdrama*, *Pygmalion*, learned by many through the musical adaptation of Lerner and Lowe's *My Fair Lady*.

As in most Shavian drama, the affluent comedy rests on serious and deep matter. On the surface it seems naive and romantically beguiled, as if the proper use of English is all that separates the fine from the vulgar, that a few lessons in phonetics can make a lady out of a flower girl. The implicit ideology seems socialist-egalitarian. Eliza—"a good girl I am"—possesses an instinctive decency that is merely muddied over with the filth of the streets, and the arrogant Higgins is blinded to her feelings by his upper-class disdain, leaving him unprepared for the metanoia the association with excellence has wrought in Eliza's soul. On this veneer, the play seems but pleasant froth, an engaging vehicle for Shaw's seductive wit. Yet, a good performance and respectful reflection show worthier resource. Once it is grasped that the phonetic training is not the cause but the parallel of Eliza's personal refinement, once the metaphoric significance replaces the social critique, the realization emerges that here is an unfolding of an educational drama that entertains in large part because of the largesse of its truth. Eliza's refinement is not due merely to her being offered opportunity, for her father, Alfred, also benefits financially, and he remains a charming but vulgar man. The title, *Pygmalion*, is from an ancient Greek myth in which the king of Cyprus sculpts a statue of a beautiful woman and then falls in love with it, begging Aphrodite to spark the stone with human life. The goddess grants his plea, and the king is now mastered by his own creation. This, of course, is the true paradox of what Plato calls a musical-gymnastic education: what seems to be our creation is in fact our reality; we do not make art and culture, but art and culture make us who we are. This is especially true of language. Refinement as education refines ourselves. To speak finely makes us fine; the common are common not because of social birth, but because as unrefined, they cannot learn who they are.

If, like the king of Cyprus, Professor Higgins "creates" Eliza the lady, in such creating he becomes enrapt to the point of idolatry; if in learning to speak finely Eliza becomes fine, she surpasses her "creator," and indeed surpasses herself. If we create art and yet learn from it, perhaps even become works of art ourselves, the paradox must be now deeply probed, not to make it unparadoxical, since no true paradox is ever resolved to the point of losing its sting, but to find in it an echo of the truth that can only be achieved by learning.

We have seen how our perceptions can be refined; now we must learn how such refining refines ourselves.

Transition

The discovery that we can refine our perceptions has broader ontological implications than is suggested merely by an aesthetics of the fine; there is a parallel between the fine perceived and the fine achieved. From our earlier reflections we learn the four following keys:

1. What we refine is meaning; the measure of refinement is the depth of penetration into meaning. If the perceived art of architecture, for example, refines and reveals what it means to dwell, it is obvious that dwelling itself, and not merely the perception of the architectural work, admits of refinement.
2. Art as refining perception probes toward essence, understood as that which makes meaning possible; that is, essence grounds meaning. *King Lear* as an artwork shows us what it means to be an unthanked father, which is grounded in the essence of being a father. Gratitude for one's existence as well as one's inheritance is meaningful because of this paternal essence. The degredation of "pelican daughters" and his own peculiar anguish at being unhonored shows us what it means for there to be daughters by showing us what it means to fail at being daughters. The essence that "grounds" such meaning—that is, which makes it possible to be meaningful as fathers and daughters—is the essence of being a father of daughters. So essence is of meanings, not of things or words.
3. This meaning is refined through art. Great artworks are cultural mirrors that reflect our reality. Since we cannot perceive ourselves directly—since we only perceive other things, given the essence of perception as receptivity—we can approach our reality only by reflection; and reflection needs reflectors or mirrors. This phenomenon of cultural reflection in the mirroring of great artworks is a part of our own meaning, not merely the meaning of what is perceived.
4. Therefore, if perception can be refined, and in this refinement the meaning of dwelling and being fathers is refined and revealed, we ourselves, and not merely our perceptions, can be refined. With the achieved enlightenment of the prior section, it is therefore possible to ask what it means to refine ourselves. So the trek of the quest proceeds from hill to mountain, from the fine perceived to the fine achieved.

The first climb is not merely an elevation, it is a foothill to a mountain. We cannot leave behind the fine perceived, as if it serves merely as an entrance. We already are refining ourselves in refining our perceptions. We not only perceive what it means to dwell in the felt receptivity of a great work of architecture, we actually refine our own meaning as dwellers; for dwelling is not a mere activity that we may or may not do; rather, we are dwellers essentially, and, hence, we succeed and fail at dwelling. It is nevertheless a steeper grade to climb when, cresting the hill we address the mountain. We do not "shift" from aesthetics to moral ontology; rather, we elevate the former to the latter by means of the climb.

What, then, does it mean to achieve the fine by means of refinement? This cannot mean to add on something new, as a synthetic proposition adds on new characteristics by the assignment of a predicate, the way "tall" tells us something new and hence not essential to the tree. If the fine is achieved through refinement, there must be some preexisting possibility or latent essence that is isolated or even extracted by the refinement. Yet, there *is* something "new"—though it is not "added on"—for the extraction or isolation itself not only shows us who we are but actually changes us in our being shown. This is called *learning* in its existential and, hence, fundamental sense. To learn, in this special sense, is not simply to acquire knowledge—indeed, it is not the acquisition of knowledge at all—but to become who we are, to achieve our meaning. To achieve the fine through refinement is therefore to become who we are essentially or, to be more precise, to become our essence. This must imply that it is possible to fail at being who we are essentially, else in achieving, we have not changed at all.

Does it make sense to speak this way? Is it possible to be "inessential" and then to become "essential"? Is having an essence not a sinecure of existence? As long as I am, it seems I must have an essence, though I may admittedly be too dull to realize what it is. Or is it the case that I can truly fail at "having" an essence? Perhaps this possessive verb "to have" harkens darkly back to the discredited metaphysics of the Enlightenment in which substances "have" properties, parallel to the indicative mode in grammar in which subjects "have" predicates. Such metaphysical isomorphism with grammar may be weakened considerably when we realize that language is far richer than that provided by the indicative mode referring to what is the case. Perhaps we should speak not of "having" essence but of "being" essence, though this substitution may seem to make it more difficult to speak about "achieving" an essence—even as it now may be easier to speak of "becoming" an essence. Yet this refinement from "having" to "being" in terms of essence, though perhaps more challenging, as a mountain is to a hill, is more elevating and provides wider vision. It suggests we can be nonessence and become, or perhaps approach, through the refinement known as learning, essence. If we retain the earlier suggestion that by essence is meant "making meaning possible," it then seems permissible, though challenging, to suggest we can become the ground of our meaning—that is, we can become our own essence—through learning to become who we are.

Such ruminations cannot wander far from the actual confrontations we have of such refinement and the lack of it. The sail of speculation is idle without the keel of experience or the rudder of critique. Yet, it is precisely in these actual confrontations that the refining language of speculation is demanded, for the keel and rudder alone do not propel the boat; the sail must be hoisted. We do indeed confront lack of essence, and it is possible to describe this phenomenon.

The Description

They seem mere shells. They possess all the external appearances of humanity; they eat and sleep, smile and frown, walk and rest. But their absence is as little noted as their presence; they are quickly forgotten, though they often leave a curious slightly sour aftertaste in the half-buried reaches of our consciousness. They are but mannequins, usurpers of our meaning, since they have no meaning themselves. Theirs is a placebo existence, lacking any improvement or benefit. For them to be is no different than for them not to be, entirely spoiling Hamlet's question.

It does no good to protest this unfairness, for we know it is so. We may misprize another thus through our prejudice, but such mistakes are the fault not of the validity of the judgments but of our bias. We know it is possible to lack meaning. We know it because it is our own possibility. We can fail, somehow, to be real; we can lack essence. Deep down, they say, they're shallow; the surface is all.

There are those entirely unrefined by art, insensitive to moral outrage, bereft of all respect for others as well as themselves, denied any judgment of their worth, purged even of their own self-contempt; though noisy they are not heard, though ubiquitous they seem not even to cast shadows.

We have been taught by recent persuaders of sameness and tolerance not to make such judgments, which, if heeded makes us not only unjudging but unjudgable. "Judge not, that you may not be judged" is a scriptural maxim that has been distorted; it is countered here, "Judge, lest you remain forever unjudged." Left in some suspended state like limbo, neither hell nor heaven, neither home nor exile, to be unable to be judged at all is worse than to be judged badly or even wrongly. As Nietzsche notes, it is better to have the void as purpose than to be void of purpose.

These who are so bereft of meaning are coarse in the extreme; they are entirely vulgar in the sense that they lack all refinement. But to identify them in this way suggests that vulgarity in the existential sense is meaninglessness. The vulgar are without shadows, they shout without being heard, they trod in the mud and leave no footprints though they may stain the carpet. To be vulgar is not to matter; it is to have no essence, no uniqueness. This is why vulgar in earlier usage was identified as "common"—lacking anything distinctive.

To refine is thus not only to achieve meaning, it is to make meaning possible. This is the tugboat that leads the freighter out of the harbor. When we speak of the fine, it seems we speak of the origin of possibility, as a fine young man offers hope of what seemed unthinkable before, or as a graceful ballerina shows us how thrilling it is to be in space, so wonderfully does she move. Prior to her grace, to be in space was a mere condition of other things; now it matters on its own. To achieve the fine is therefore to become the origin of meaning: it is to become essence, or even to have essence, in the colloquial syntax. By becoming essence in becoming fine, we make meaning possible.

This philosophical language may seem demanding or even arcane, but the real confrontations are true enough. It is foolish indeed to pretend there are no differences between the vulgar and the fine: there are those whose vulgarity offends just because it offers nothingness, and there are the fine, whose presence enables learning to be possible by revealing meaning. To play the monkey who, covering his eyes, sees no evil, and to sacrifice this palpable distinction on the altar of egalitarian sameness is self-deception at its most vulgar. These judgments are real; to gainsay their authority is petulant delusion. It is their concrete, irresistible urgency that yokes us to the burden of this quest, for we escape it only by self-eclipse. The harsh, brute, implacable reality, truer than our knowledge that a dozen halved is a pair tripled, is that our own existence can be fine or vulgar, that who we are either matters or lacks meaning. These are direct experiences, like Hume's impressions; they cannot go away though we can deceive ourselves by turning away from them. Granted there are the fine and the vulgar, then what does it mean? How do we think about this presupposition? Such thinking is called learning.

Learning

Learning can be understood in two ways. A schoolchild learns by assimilating information from lectures and texts, but the same child learns to play the violin by practice, becoming a musician. Though these are distinct, they obviously overlap: the rote assimilation of famous dates may prepare the way to become a historian, and the violin playing may well produce factual knowledge of the names of notes, clefs, and keys. Nevertheless, it is the difference that matters here, for just as the actual practice of the scales, tedious though it may be, is understood as preparing the child to *play* the violin and ultimately to *become* a musician, and not merely to achieve propositional knowledge of which notes are which, so the fundamental learning by refinement is understood as making possible our becoming who we are. The development of a skill, which may even lead to the achievement of being a musician, is closer to existential learning than is the mere accumulation of knowledge by receiving information. It is possible then to suggest we learn to be. This daunting language of the ontologist may be rendered less obtuse by reflection on what it means to say we can learn to become who we are. The term *becoming* emphasizes our temporal finitude, and the phrase "who we are" suggests not our present state, but a constant and abiding focus or essence that is achieved through refinement. Even so, the central discovery is that *what* is learned is not knowledge of something else, but what it means to be, so that the realm of discourse is the meaning of being. Since we are fundamentally temporal, the meaning of our being is becoming, and so the addendum can be concretized by the formulation: "becoming who we are." This formulation also allows us to recognize in the present tense, "are," the refinement in such learning, working, as it were, on what is already there as a beckoning to achieve what is fine, and hence what is real, for the real is here understood as the ground of the true.

The analogy with learning to play the violin as a way of becoming a musician can be pressed. There are discordant, unpleasant, even outright offensive sounds that come from unrefined playing prior to the practice that changes the student from nonplayer to musician. Even at the beginning of the very first lesson, the student winces painfully at the sour shrieks that emanate from early attempts, so that he knows first there is success and failure—there are bad sounds and good sounds to be elicited from the stringed wooden box—which originate his willingness to discipline and refinement; he wants to avoid the harsh and vulgar sounds and to be able to produce the sweet and compelling ones. In the same way, we first realize that our becoming can succeed or fail, and then we seek to achieve success at becoming who we are, as the tyro practices to become a musician. What is learned is refinement; hence, to be fine is the lesson learned. Since I already exist, I cannot learn to exist, but I can learn what it means to exist. I do not begin with a grasp of the essence that makes such meaning possible, it is achieved; and what makes the achievement possible is the difference between being common—in the sense that, merely as a member of a species my own uniqueness makes no difference at all—and being fine, in which my own uniqueness not only matters but in turn illuminates, by mirrored reflection of the lights that reveal meaning, the essence of the species as well as myself. Thus, learning is not the accumulation of factual knowledge, for such acquisition in no way refines, but is rather a becoming that rests upon the unfolding of a narrative or storylike development in which a themed character or essence emerges. This emerging essence is not arbitrary or random, for I can succeed or fail at achieving it. On the other hand, neither is it predetermined, as some natural telos or divinely established goal. Though I may inherit some natural disposition or tendency to develop along certain lines by the genetic determinations of my DNA, providing natural propensities for certain behavior, such is not what is meant by achieving refinement of my essence, for if that were the case, there would not be true sense of success or failure. Deviations of the natural, genetic instincts could be thwarted by external trauma—the budding musician could be deafened by disease or his hands mangled in farm machinery—but this would merely be the frustration of physical development not existential failure; and the natural maturing of bodily similarities to one's parents would not be success but simply fulfillment of corporeal laws. To speak of success and failure as necessary for learning who one is cannot be accounted for by inherited physical propensities or external traumas that frustrate corporeal development.

It is perhaps harder to deny that a divine providence determines success and failure, though it is equally difficult to affirm it, since in either case the appeal is made to magnificently appalling ignorance. If we are divinely provided, however, there simply can be no meaningful sense of failure or success, since, if it stems from divine agency the fault is not ours, and the failure, being writ by divine hand, is really success in disguise. There may be divine promise in the sense that, given the talents to succeed as a great musician, I frustrate God's plan by indolence or a perverse distraction to wicked ways; but in such a case the success or failure is still my own, though the essence would somehow have the handwork of God in its making. These theological speculations, however, lie beyond the blinkered vision of philosophical inquiry and, in any event, make no difference to what is fundamental. The point remains that we can refine ourselves in terms of our essence, or we can remain idle and, hence, common or vulgar, merely taking up space in the ample width of the species.

These pathoempirical descriptions of essence-failure draw attention to existential learning, in which the very process of refinement rather than some unachievable goal or unreached end achieves essence as the ground of meaning. By these reflections on what it is like to be without meaning, it is possible to elicit some profound hints of what it is like to become meaningful. It is crucial that learning—which is the process or development of what it means to become essence—not be seen as some static state and, hence, neither as the acquisition of knowledge nor the complete development of a skill. If it is possible to exist in such a way as to lack essence and to have no meaning, it must also be possible to become in such a way as to achieve meaning. The grammatic shift from the infinitival "to exist" to the infinitival "to become" is fundamental, for the focus no longer is on a state but on a development. This development is learning, but always in a peculiarly unfolding sense, as a story unfolds it meanings.

This appeal to the truth-unfolding of a story is more than merely metaphoric. Stories do explain but they also happen; we can tell a true story of an actual life or historical development and through the telling learn its meaning. The story is not a mere vehicle that links discrete events, as if the events themselves are true and real, whereas the storied linkage is but a method to discover them. Rather, it is the story that is true and real, from which the events, as elements of it, take their meaning. If this be so, then the elements of storytelling—or perhaps, if we are allowed some latitude: story-learning—become necessary to our quest. In seeking to understand what it means to achieve the fine, we have discovered that this achieving, as a way of becoming, unfolds as a story. So we must tell the story of how stories are told.

Whoever told the first story launched the race toward its meaning. From those whose task it is to reflect and remark on this semidivine activity of storytelling—far greater than the discovery of causal connections—we learn that stories have three elements: plot, theme, and character. The plot and theme may seem the most obvious, even aboriginal, but it is character that most distinguishes the successful from the unsuccessful story. The absolutely silly plots of some of Shakespeare's comic plays are made into wondrous achievements of the highest art by his splendid characters. We remember who Cleopatra is long after we have forgotten—if we ever did figure out—the political complexities of the bewildering plot. In fact, under the influence of his genius, the plot is often misprized and deliberately demoted, as when, in the prologue to *Romeo and Juliet*, he tells us everything that will happen so that the plot has no suspense or even interest. The theme, on the other hand, is often murky as a concept, though always vivid as felt. Learned scholars may wrangle endlessly in precious and honored disputation on the themes of great works; but it is their very elusiveness that makes them unfit for the crown announcing the sovereignty among the elements. This royal title belongs to character. It is as character that we are manifested in the meaning of who we are to become. It is, indeed, in the unfolding of the character that the theme is developed and revealed; and it is because this themed character matters that the plot rivets our attention.

It must be made clear what this term means; and it may be helpful to locate it in terms of the fundamental distinctions as to how we think about ourselves. Within the realm of nature, I am both *caused* and *cause*: I am caused by the biological union of my parents and, when sitting on the couch, I am the cause of the indentation of the cushion. Within the realm of moral action, I am agent. I am, as guilty, responsible for my actions and am consequently held accountable for them. To break a promise is to incur the censure of my own reason, and thus, as agent I have moral worth and as the author of the precepts that govern such judgment, I can demand respect. But in the unfolding of my story, I am more than mere cause or agent; I am character. To be character, as opposed to cause or agent, is to be meaningful, that is, thinkable in terms of success and failure; and as the ultimate essence of such meaning, I have existential, and not merely moral, worth. To say I am a cause is to put me in the linear connectedness of events, which allows me to be thought of as object; to be an agent is to attribute moral responsibility to me, which entails the ascription of praise or censure as an actor or performer of deeds; to be character is to be thinkable in terms of developing toward essence, and thus not only to be meaningful but also to be the nonrelative origin of meaning. The first demands that what kind of thing I am matters, and the second that what I do matters. The third, however, demands that *who I am becoming* matters.

In ordinary discourse this becoming is often loosely described as a life. We speak about "the life of King John" meaning "the story of King John"; or we read of pre-Enlightenment figures receiving moral education by reading the "Lives of the Saints." To read the lives of the saints was not meant as an entertainment, but as a spiritual elevation, for it was believed that to learn of these saintly lives was to learn what it means to be spiritual. Lives, in this educative sense, meant far more than the mere account of a biological phenomenon but were intended rather as a biographical unfolding. These brief reflections show that this traditional understanding of a life is indeed an understanding of a story. The terms are almost interchangeable, so that a life itself now has a theme, a character, and a plot, although plot is in this context often supplanted with destiny.

The habit of reading the lives of the saints may seem quaint to the modern mind, but what it reveals about learning is of considerable importance. It is only in the telling of saintly stories that we learn what a saint is; and if being a saint is a meaningful notion, then so, too, are the metaphysical presuppositions that provide the kind of world in which saints can exist. The ancients told stories of heroes, and only through such telling did we learn about the metaphysical and moral universe that makes heroes possible. Hence, the telling of these stories is prior, both formally and temporally, to their metaphysics. The lives of saints and heroes, kings and artists, teachers and sufferers are told, as stories are told; and in their unfolding we discover essence. Even if the story itself is of unsuccess, as in tragedy for example, or of great suffering, like the story of the holocaust, the very unfolding reveals meaning and, hence, success and failure. Tragic heroes are still heroes and sinning saints are still saints: Peter's threefold denial of Christ is a saint's denial, and Othello's unsuccess as warrior-lover is still that of a hero. Even if we attempt to tell the story of a mediocre, common man as Arthur Miller says he does of Willy Loman, the attempt is frustrated, for insofar as the play *Death of a Salesman* succeeds, his theory of it fails. Willy is not just common, he is a loser and not, as Miller later argued, a victim. The loser reveals victory as much as the victor. Willy's dream may be misguided, and his lonely struggles unappreciated, but in the telling of it, the dreams are still dreams and his ignobility is but unsuccess of the noble.

If by the term *life* we mean simply whatever happens to anyone between birth and death, it is not obvious that life is meaningful, certainly not that this life is equally meaningful to that one. A mere listing of the events between birth and death is not a story; and not all who have gone from birth to death have lived tellable lives. To chronicle the passage of uninteresting events that occur in the duration of a characterless subject can never provide a story. A gifted artist may take a seemingly arid existence and infuse it with life, not by altering the events but by changing the subject to a character. However, this merely shows that character is sovereign in the kingdom of tales.

To inquire into character is to inquire into essence. If, by studying the text carefully and watching the drama performed, I can learn the character of Prospero, I am at the same time learning the essence of *The Tempest*. By studying the told history or life of Abraham Lincoln, I can appreciate the essence of the civil struggle that remade America, and if I study the unfolding drama of my own life, I can discern the essence or character of my own reality—though in this last case, since the story must remain incomplete, my learning remains an unfinished task. If there is little character in my own dramatic unfolding, there is little to think about; and, hence, not only are there interesting and uninteresting stories and lives, within one story there may be possible successes and failures at being character.

This emphasis upon the inequality of lives and stories is necessary, though it may seem unfair, because unless there are these unequal differences, there is no sense of success or failure as a story. Hence, there is no meaning or essence that makes the meaning possible. Perhaps every story is at least minimally tellable, so that no actual life is entirely bereft of any and all meaning, but that is of little comfort to the learner; for if indeed what we learn is to become who we are becoming—and not to become who we must become—then learning refines and indolent nonlearning coarsens.

More precisely, the lesson learned is always truth; even though it is noted above that what is learned is the fine. These are not two conflicting accounts, since to be fine is to achieve and to radiate essence, and truth is always of essence. Learning truth is therefore a form of refinement, perhaps the essential refinement.

What does it mean to speak of a fine young man? The image can be approached by social appearances, recognizing that these may not be essential in themselves, but nevertheless provide some initiary purchase on the phenomenon. The young man is fine if he speaks properly, says "please" and "thank you," and is generally polite and mannerly. He is attractive, clean, decent, and honorable. Yet, he is not a mere obedient slave of custom, for he has spirit, and because of this spirit he has promise. We expect fine things to come from this fine young man, and so his presence excites a sense of our future, letting what is important have an advocate in the arriving generation. We are grateful that he represents a way of existing, which in turn includes his own gratitude for the inheritance that makes him a fine young man. He is therefore an image *in media res*, a character in the midst of his unfolding drama, with a cultural past giving him advantage and a richly promising future providing hope. There is in this image an ache of transcience lurking in this bloom of youth, stamped with the destiny of origin and the lure of brightening dawns. The hope rooted in the soil of legacy is not that he merely affords a link in our cultural chain, passing what is precious on to the unborn, but that in his hungry absorption of its nectar, he will unfold, as a blossom unfolds, newer and in wider radiance, seeking sunlight energy to expand what is noble, even as it stretches toward wilt, decay, and rot. It is the promise that brightens, a promise rooted in an ancient, fecund soil.

Can these elitist fineries such as good manners and proper speech really matter that much? Are not the socially victimized insulted by this image? Is not a tough ghetto youth, whose language is shredded with obscenities and whose hunger for unearned wealth and justice is sated entirely without thanks or grace, equally deserving—perhaps even more deserving because of his victimization? Is not the proposition stating equality among all the finest and noblest creed uttered by the human tongue? If it is noble to claim the equality of all, is it not ignoble to rank at all? This we know is but a coarse and vulgar reading of this great proposition, for an equality of rights provides an opportunity for the achievement of what is fine—it does not render the fine as common. That all citizens are equal before the law is an ennobling judgment, not a base one. To press the social fabric to allow a ghetto youth to become a fine young man cannot imply the denial of the difference between the fine and the vulgar, for that would debase the equality principle to a principle of the lowest common denominator. To be born equal is not to die equal; a republican government, muted by democracy, protects the right to learn and to become who we are; and in this protection we let the fine become possible.

This chapter's reflections began not with a fine young man, but with a vulgar young girl, Eliza Doolittle, who through learning her own language, became a fine young lady. To speak beautifully renders us beautiful, and beauty is the finest educator. Henry Higgins himself learns who he is; like the ancient Greek Pygmalion he learns to worship his own creation, and even to become enslaved by it, suggesting that to create is simply to mirror our own becoming. There is a distinction in education between providing information (the Latin *docere*—teaching) and extracting truth (*ex-ducere*: to lead out—education). This distinction between teaching and educating is helpful; but like all such distinctions can be overemphasized to the point of distortion. It is a false dichotomy, for in many ways to put into a soul (*docere*) is to extract from a soul (*ex-ducere*), and all extraction is a kind of putting into. Distinctions are insidious without a synthesizing unity; both teaching and education are simply variations of self-refining in which we become who we are in part by letting our own stories happen. We refine ourselves to become fine.

Chapter 5

The Gracious

One of the most troubling yet necessary distinctions in philosophy is between the moral and the aesthetic; what is beautiful need not always be good and what is moral need not be beautiful. Yet the distinction, if too severely drawn, seems to eclipse one of the more important domains of the fine. It seems entirely cogent to suggest that to refine who we are, which begins aesthetically with refinement of our perceptions, should also make us morally better persons. The experiential evidence that not all who are refined are morally improved in no way mutes the voice that would persuade us it is good to refine and be refined. Indeed, that the fine are not always good provides a special kind of anguish that is itself revealing. In the sixty-seventh sonnet, the poet cries out: "Ah, wherefore with infection should he live,/ And with his presence grace impiety,/ That sin by him advantage should achieve/ And lace itself with his society?" The infection decried in the first line is moral, not physical. The anguish is not a mere personal disappointment but also a universal, antinomic frustration with the shaling of the stony idol, cracking the solid synthesis of the beautiful with the good. It is as if imperfections in the fine not only disappoint but also scandalize.

Scandal offends the good more deeply than moral wrong, for as scandal it vexes the public conscience, unanchors the lighted beacons from their moorings, and leaves us to toss rudderless on heaving and erratic seas. This moral confusion is an entirely unenviable state, for in it the strategies of restoration are lost, and our natural weaknesses are made more dangerous since they are bereft of any guidance. When the fine and the radiant become corrupt, the stain widens beyond the limits of fault, precisely because the fine already extends beyond itself in its universalizing power. In the couplet of another sonnet, ninety-four, Shakespeare sees this with horrific clarity: "Sweetest things turn sourest by their deeds;/ Lilies that fester smell far worse than weeds."

It would seem, therefore, that though there may be an aesthetics of the fine there cannot be an ethics of the fine, since being fine does not always imply being good. At the same time, since scandal is a moral notion, there seems to be moral capital in refinement, so the dismissive ease of disjoining the fine from the good is treacherous. The poet's expression of universal anguish at seeing his beloved do wicked things reveals that the fine is not entirely separate from the good, else the moral failure of the fine would not evoke such torment. Scandal disappoints our expectations that the radiant should be constant. We are not scandalized when the base do wicked things, for that is their nature. The fact we are scandalized at all—which occurs only when the esteemed have fallen—shows this disposition to see in the fine a champion of goodness. Kant goes so far as to describe the beautiful as the form of the morally good, thereby linking the aesthetic with the moral in a way that allows for the beautiful not always being good, though in its beauty it yet shows us what being good means. Kant's argumentation for this is tortuous and profound, but strikes a familiar chord. It is not enough merely to claim a certain psychological fact, that when we perceive the fine we merely *feel* there is goodness inherent in it. The flawless feminine beauty on the face of the Virgin in Michelangelo's *Pietà* is not merely a pleasant addendum to our understanding of that work; the exquisite, motherly tenderness seems aesthetically appropriate to the holiness of the scene. It is naive to believe that those who have lovely faces also must have lovely characters, but it is not naive, indeed, it is profoundly coherent, to see in the loveliness of the one a formal mirroring of the loveliness of what the other ought to be.

The stable, on witnessing the fall of the noble, need not become entirely wanton in conduct. Scandal does not always result in the collapse of moral rectitude, for we retain our own responsibility for who we are; but the unfathomable sadness that follows such violation reveals that the fine and the good are not radically distinct but somehow belong together.

These reflections are profoundly disturbing. They assault some of our deepest instincts of fairness and justice. For the suggestion here is that there are a few rather special persons who, though not always good, seem to embody the meaning of goodness; that when they err their failures are more offensive and culpable than others. To say lilies that fester smell worse than weeds opens a daring possibility. Are there those few whose virtue exceeds in worth the same virtue found in most others, whose faults glare with fiercer censure than most others? It seems both ideologically and ethically outrageous to suggest it; yet it seems to fly in the face of reality to deny it. This seems to be one of the most enduring characteristics of the fine; almost, one might say, the essence of the fine: that their sins are not just sins but, because they are perpetrated by the fine, are sacrilege and that their virtues are not mere dispositions for good behavior but are sacred, radiating to the rest of us the light of the remarkable. This is fair neither to them nor to us, but we deny it only by making the common and the vulgar our standard, thereby debasing ourselves.

Nothing abets this debasement more than to reduce it to peculiar psychological feelings, accounting for it by the natural phenomenon of erotic bondage. When the poet falls in love, he is caught in the grip of a curious and amusing slavery, demeaning himself before an idealized perfection of his beloved that goes unnoticed by the rest of the world. This reduces the poet's anguish to the psychological mechanism by which the species is propogated, no more or less noteworthy than any other comical aspect of human procreation. True, those smitten do idolize their less-than-ideal loves, a phenomenon that perhaps deserves a comic response, as Silvius's pure love for the uncomely Phebe evokes our warm, affirming laughter, but from this we do not extract the dreadful reverence suggested by sonnet ninety-four. Phebe is not Cleopatra; Silvius is not Marc Antony.

The fine is neither the beautiful nor the good; but neither is it entirely distinct from them or unrelated to them. Perhaps there is no "ethics of the fine" in the strict sense that the fine either is equated with or explains the good; but it can be manifested in those singular virtues that inspire a sense of respect for refinement. If we provisionally accept the reality of the elegant few who, in their nobility, seem to matter more in their sins and triumphs, it is possible to examine what this means by reflection on the phenomenon of the gracious.

When Orlando, with sword drawn, first confronts the senior duke in the forest of Arden, he does so saucily, provoking the duke's remonstration: "Art thou thus bolden'd, man, by thy distress:/ Or else a rude despiser of good manners,/ That in civility thou seem'st so empty?" (*As You Like It* II, 7). When Orlando explains his need for food, the duke continues his graceful reprimand: "your gentleness shall force/ More than your force move us to gentleness," and bids Orlando sit down and eat. The noble youth is shamed by this: "Speak you so gently? Pardon me I pray you:/ I thought all things had been savage here; . . . Let gentleness my strong enforcement be:/ In the which hope I blush, and hide my sword."

This scene is a masterpiece of grace, for it not only tells us that gentility outranks force, it shows us what it means to be gracious. It is easy to be misled by this scene; the point made is not simply that politeness always disarms the savage, for that is false. Nor does it mean the mere exercise of good etiquette guarantees success. Such arguments mislead by justifying grace by its consequences. The scene deserves more respectful scrutiny than to find in it pious social maxims.

Orlando's appearance is itself remarkable; he draws his sword against the entire group of the duke's armed men who, if Jacques is any model, are more amused by his boldness than intimidated. His daring may be in part explained by his extreme youth, his hunger, and his moral responsibility to succor the gentle Adam; but it also speaks of courage, and the duke senses that his reprimand will not fall on unhearing ears. When called, the youth is ashamed of this brash appeal to force. However, it is the duke's behavior that illuminates the scene. Perhaps he recognizes instantly something of Orlando's quality, but in any event, his graciousness is decisive. It contrasts vividly with the ungracious ducal usurper who now, through force alone, rules the court; at the same time it provides the meaning of the title. This is how we like the world to be—not only where comically beguiled fools in love ultimately triumph, for that is the stuff of all the comedies, but also where the gracious produces such an atmosphere of fond, warm dignity we cannot resist the induced judgment that this is As You Like It.

It may be tempting to mute the efficacy of this by pointing out that the duke's gentility is in fact backed by power; he still has his little army with him, and prior to his defeat by his cruel brother was accustomed to security and prestige. It is easy to be gracious when one is well armed, well fed, and well esteemed. That, however, is precisely the point. Grace, in its truest sense, does flow from abundance, but abundance in itself need not always produce grace, as is manifested by the preconversion characters of the usurping Duke Frederick and Orlando's brother Oliver. Superiority in rank can produce simple terror or envy, it can be the basis of scandal, or it can be gracious. But grace itself seems to flow from affluence, whether of natural beauty, of power, or simply of noble character. What is remarkable about grace is that it seeds itself in bestowal, making the receptive also graceful.

In this it is the true counterpoint to scandal, in which, because of affluence, the sin becomes the seed for further sins; so in grace the virtue is similarly spread. It is infectious, like scandal, not because the receptive are imitative of beneficence, but because gratitude itself is a species of abundance. This infectious quality can be discerned in the genealogy of the central characters. Orlando's late father is marked as both noble and gracious by others in the play, and his offspring manifest this inheritance, though in Oliver's case his nobility is darkened by unseemly envy for his brother's charm and is discovered only when he submits to the forgiving magic of the forest of Arden. The loyal servant Adam, whose "service sweat(s) for duty, not for mead!" seems remarkably generous, giving Orlando the hoarded gold of his long years, and yet receives from him a loving loyalty in return. The senior duke finds meaning even in the adversity of the forest, and his own offspring, Rosalind, graces everyone with her spirit. The forest of Arden teems enchantedly with grace, where everything is as you like it precisely because of all the gracious inhabitants. Even the shameless, like Phebe and Touchstone, yield to this magic of the generous, if only out of self-interest if not self-esteem.

Grace is contrasted with force, but it also contrasts with the strict and the moral, as if goodness itself cannot alone produce the gracious. This insight allows a tentative description. If Kant is right, the essence of moral goodness is respect for the moral law and, by inference, respect for all who can by reason originate that law. Respect for others, when made beautiful, is graciousness. The duke's welcome of Orlando is not merely respectful, it is also fine; his remonstrance is stern but gentle. Grace consists of doing one's duty in a way that makes it acceptable, even joyous, by transcending the mere moral requirement, making it fine. Since it is morally required merely to do one's duty and not necessarily to do one's duty graciously, grace itself is supererogatory. By reading Kant's moral works, we may come to realize that we must respect all moral agents, but by witnessing a performance of *As You Like It*, we see that the gracious somehow embodies or perhaps reflects the meaning of respect itself.

There are external manifestations of grace, such as gentility in language and demeanor, etiquette, politeness, generosity, and compassion. Though these are social virtues that can be mere developed skills that charm for advantage, even so, long practice in such behavior may well refine character, so that the impulse to act in such overtly refined ways stems not from self-interest but self-esteem. It is misleading to draw too severely the public etiquette from the true refinement of character, for this exaggerates the sharp metaphysical distinction between the subject and the world. The world, if properly conceived, must contain the subject, and the subject is always already in the world, never outside it looking in. It is helpful, therefore, to say that the gracious is duty manifested beautifully; but by saying this the sharp cleavage between the good and the beautiful is muted. The distinction must perforce persist, but not to the point of absolute disjunction.

Perhaps then there can be an "ethics of the fine," not in the reductionist sense of defining the former in terms of the latter but in the realization that respect for the law must to some extent itself be respected. To say that "good manners," when grounded in respect and made beautiful by grace, are virtues is to grant wider appeal to the ethical concerns for living a rich and meaningful life than the more precise but narrower concerns of the moralist to act according to the proper maxim. If grace itself is a virtue, perhaps it may be possible to speak of an ethics of the fine but not a morality of the fine.

Grace seems supererogatory in another sense, insofar as it is thought a bestowal. To be gracious is to grant above and beyond what is earned, which may invite the censure of unfairness but nonetheless can be affirmed, as gifts can be affirmed, because they celebrate not our moral action but more profoundly who we are. Being gracious triumphs the worth and meaning of existence itself, which is why the recipient of grace is grateful. Strictly, we do not thank the giver of what we earn, for it is ours by right; we thank only when the bestowal is given on the basis of favor that can never be universalized. Grace particularizes in a way that mere justice cannot, for to treat another justly is to treat as one ought to treat everyone, but to be gracious is to affirm and isolate the uniqueness of the recipient. Gratitude, as the response to grace, likewise honors uniqueness, both in the recipient and in the donor. I cannot be grateful merely for morally proper conduct, for that is demanded by reason and is universal; but I can be grateful for the graciousness with which this moral duty is offered. Yet, to couch the moral in the raiment of grace seems more than a mere addendum; it seems rather to let the moral shine through its truth; that ungraced, the good is merely done not embraced.

What would it mean to act morally but ungraciously, to perform as we ought but to do so in a manner that makes the performance distasteful? Would it be good at all? We suffer genuine distress when puritanical severity sours its own good deeds, for we thereby sense an alienation from goodness. Kant's claim that true moral worth lies solely in willing actions for the sake of duty seems at first reading to make such sour puritanism not only possible but perhaps even mandatory—a reading that so inflames Schopenhauer that he announces it a hideous doctrine. So conceived, Kant's position may indeed be hideous, but it is not necessary to read such dour meaning into it. Perhaps true respect for the moral law requires the law to be respected and not merely obeyed, which in turn requires that it be noble as well as authoritative. However, this would seem to require that we be gracious as well as dutiful, which would in effect make grace simply another duty, entirely subverting the fundamental distinction.

The dilemma may be eased, though not entirely erased, by recognizing that it is one thing to do what is good and quite another to be good; but this merely complicates the issue with another distinction. The glory of the gracious is to wed these distinct qualities into a union of sacramental power. Curiously, to disjoin the gracious from the good, souring morality as it were, is itself a form of scandal, which has two faces. The more familiar is that lamented in Shakespeare's sixty-seventh sonnet, in which the beloved's beauty seems to grace the wicked; but it is equally scandalous to present the good in such foul attire that association with it seems ugly. To act morally but ungraciously thus scandalizes just as dreadfully as to act immorally but with such grace that we are addled in our judgment. To say we *ought* to be both gracious and moral, though perhaps true enough in one sense, puts us in an unsavory predicament; for if grace is morally required, it simply is not grace any more. It is far more accurate to say it is fine to be moral graciously. If there is an echo of an ought in this, it is of a different breed more akin to the judgment that Mozart selects the one, perfect note that "ought" to be played at that moment.

To be gracious concretizes the fine; it sacrifices personal interest for the sake of manifested respect, particularizing by favor, which by definition is not universal, that which mirrors universality. Only the few can be favored—for such elitist selection is entailed in the term—but this favoring serves as a refined paradigm that gives meaning to all. Only one boy, Arthur, can pull the sword from the stone, but every boy who reads or hears the tale learns from it the universal preciousness of being a boy.

With no little caution, following Kant's lead, we may now suggest that morality is the universal applied to the particular, and beauty is the concrete raised to the level of the universal. Such formal accounts, though surely helpful, cannot constitute the explanation needed. These reflections, however, may help to bring percision to the problem. At the outset of this chapter, it is noted that the necessarily drawn distinction between the good and the beautiful, if left unconjoined, frustrates the attempt to grasp the fine, since the fine seems to partake of both. An appeal was made to find some overlap in the phenomenon of the gracious, in which the good is concretized as meaningful. This allows us to rephrase the question in broader terms, and to ask a pair: What is the worth of being good? What is the worth of being beautiful? In this questioning, both the good and the fair are seen as species of the genus, worth. Where does "worth" come from? To be gracious is to treat others as well as oneself as being worthwhile; so grace elicits worth.

Worth must be distinguished from value in exactly the same way that truth must be distinguished from opinion; the latter is subjective, the former nonarbitrary. (I avoid "objective" because of its ambiguity.) As Othello's base Indian throws a pearl away richer than all his tribe, we recognize the Indian values the pearl less than its real worth; values may change but worth is constant. To ask, then, about the worth of the good and the beautiful is to allow for their difference even as their axiological sameness in being of worth is affirmed. The concrete phenomenon manifesting this sameness or overlap is graciousness. The duke's gracious welcome of the unruly Orlando recognizes the worth of the youth; and perhaps to some extent, this recognition actually refines it, as when the surly, being treated graciously, become gracious. In any event, the phenomenon of the gracious is the reflective mirror in which we see the truth that who we are matters. To treat people as if they matter, even if such treatment may seem undeserved by the appearance of unruly behavior, is to be gracious. Thus, that we matter—or, if you will, that we have worth—is the sponsor of the gracious judgment.

The parallel between truth and opinion with worth and value is here made crucial. There is a tendency, in seeming ascendence in our present cultural climate, to seek solutions to all our social ills by the development of what might be called "achieved indifference." Under this rubric, to alleviate the blight of racism we claim that race does not matter, to avoid religious strife we assert that religion does not matter, to quell gender insensitivity we claim gender does not matter, to alleviate the burden of judgment we claim that responsibility no longer applies, so that even behavior does not matter. Since arguments about the truth cause strife, truth does not matter, and opinions are all equally ranked. However, racial injustice is cruel precisely because race does matter; religions, if meaningful at all, must matter greatly; respect for marriage and family requires that genders be profoundly different, and not merely in their silhouettes; and morality is possible only if conduct matters. Disputes about opinions are important because truth itself matters. To placate the outrage of social stress by seeking refuge in indifference ultimately forfeits both the worth and the meaning of everything, including the merry innocence of taking joy in life, and even worse, the worth of truth itself, since truth is now seen as entirely devoid of weight. Grace is the exact opposite to this nihilistic, puritanical grimness, for it refuses to deny worth even when it appears lacking, as Don Quixote refuses to treat the peasant girl, now yclept Dulcinea, in any other way except as a lady, which moves her to become ladylike. That the don dwells in fantasy does not forfeit his grace any more than the fiction of the story forfeits its truth.

When we are treated graciously, we are esteemed as being worthwhile, perhaps even worthier than we deserve. This phenomenon may be explained away in terms solely restricted to psychological feelings and, hence, seemingly of little value for the philosophical inquirer. But feeling worthwhile raises the question of being worthwhile, which gives the gracious phenomenon philosophical significance. Gracious treatment does not merely mean that the gracious one values who we are, for that may be an entirely subjective appraisal; it also shows what it means to be of worth. Worth is the basis, not the result, of judgment. It is possible, and perhaps even helpful, to list vernacular equivalents: to be of worth is to have weight, to make a difference, to be important, to demand respect, to deserve esteem, to be of intrinsic significance, when to be at all is more fundamental than not to be. To be of worth is to say that the world itself is somehow diminished by being absent from it, whereas to be unworthy is to absent the world indifferently. Helpful as these equivalences may be, however, when pressed the series becomes circular. The reach for fundamental or simple terms, intuitively nonreducible, frustrates. It is similar to seeking a "better" term to define "up." To unpack the meaning inherent in the phenomenon of being gracious, however, has the advantage of concrete analysis. For when we are treated graciously, we not only *feel* worthy, we are made aware of what it means, or would mean, to *be* worthy.

It is therefore remarkable that we can ask what the worth of goodness and beauty is, for such asking ranks the existential modality of being of worth above the moral concern with being good and the aesthetic concern with being beautiful. It is precisely because we can imagine something of absolute worth, namely beauty, not being morally good, and something else of absolute worth, namely goodness, not being aesthically beautiful, that "being of worth" ranks as the fundamental basis of judgment. Mere definitional refinement or reduction of the term *worth* is of limited utility; and so we must seek a concrete phenomenon in which being of worth is embedded—graciousness. The gracious, however, is but a species of the fine.

If to be gracious is to treat one as important and as having worth, even if such treatment is undeserved, this inquiry into the fine has now reached an entirely new plateau. For in unpacking the phenomenon of the gracious as bestowing worth, we thereby recognize the possibility of being of worth and, hence, of being meaningful. This, however, is to confront nihilism directly, not in a mere calculative way, but concretely. Just as skepticism is confronted, not by fantastic attempts to show that certain self-referential propositions must be known as true, but concretely by dwelling in the world successfully as knowers and doubters—that is, showing that to know, to err, and to be ignorant are meaningfully distinct ways to be and to act—so nihilism is confronted by the concrete existential difference between being meaningful and being meaningless. There is in the nihilistic approach of achieved indifference a reluctance to accept the judgment that anyone can be meaningless—that deep down everyone is equally meaningful—thereby rendering the very judgment itself meaningless. Unless it is possible to be wrong, it is meaningless to say we are right; and it is also true that to be meaningful must entail the possibility of being meaningless, else the term simply dissipates like steam vanishing into the air. The skeptic is beguiled by his own knowledge of his ignorance, not realizing that to be proven wrong must assert what is right. Because he errs at times when he is unaware of his error, he insists that any given moment can be erroneously judged, and, hence, there can never be present certainty and therefore no knowledge ever, since ever consists of an infinite series of present uncertainties. That this assessment itself judges a specific moment's error from the wider perspective of extended learning seems to escape him, for the claim I may now be in error cannot extend dubiety beyond this moment, else the judgment that I err could never be learned. In the same way, the claims of being meaningful entirely disjoined from the possibility of being meaningless are simply empty, and it is into this emptiness that the unwary nihilist falls.

Ideological egalitarianism imposed a priori on judgments of worth and meaning is not only formally invalid, it disarms thought entirely, replacing the critical with a pious indifference. To be meaningful entails being able to be meaningless, and since both are possibilities, what matters is to distinguish them. Treating someone graciously is to treat one as meaningful, and treating someone ungraciously is to treat one as bereft of meaning; hence, to find out what "being meaningful" is can best be approached by an analysis of what is contained in the pathoempirical phenomena of grace and rudeness. If graciousness and rudeness are the decisive phenomena in which meaning and indifference are imbedded, such analysis may be the premier approach and possibly the only approach. Since both goodness and beauty are specific in their coverage of worth, the broader reaches of the fine as a resource for understanding meaning may well entail the legitimacy and perhaps even superiority of this inquiry.

The duke, at Orlando's surly entrance, treats him as having worth, for he chides him precisely on that basis. There is even a practical lesson here instructing us how best to chide, by pointing out that improper behavior is simply inconsistent with one's existential rank. "Remember who you are!" is the finest way to scold, for it evokes both pride and shame; pride in our belonging and shame in our self-imposed exile from that belonging. Such scolding treats one graciously even as it shames. To chide merely by spotting the error and not the nobility to overcome it is ungracious and even unhelpful because of its effect. Orlando, graciously chided, is nobly, not basely, shamed, for the duke's remonstrance appeals to the existential worth of the youth as the basis for refinement. Only in this way can Orlando restore his own esteem. What, then, does it mean to "treat as worthy"? It is to confront our shared dwelling and belonging as capable of success or failure. It is therefore *not* to place the origin of worth in the arbitrary esteem of others, as if gracious behavior merely makes us feel good; it is rather to realize the possibility of failure and success. It is not admirable simply to be admired, but to be admired because we are admirable.

This capability of success and failure presupposes the nonarbitrary status of both: we are not first free, and then because we are free we can succeed or fail. It is entirely the other way around: the reality of success and failure grounds our capacity for being free. To treat as worthy (to be gracious) thus unites our own worth with the worth of the treated, thereby confronting our belonging and our dwelling. The isolated individual seeking morality solely within his or her own personal will is hereby surpassed in the recognition that the gracious welcomes, just as the ungracious exiles, and being ungracious exiles one's self. For this deserves emphasis: the duke welcomes Orlando in his graciousness. Welcome, as opposed to exile, invites a shared belonging in such a way as to affirm the worth of dwelling. It is this ambiance of welcome that gives *As You Like It* its irresistible charm, where fool and sage, good dukes and bad dukes, lovers rejected and lovers accepted, all belong together in the welcome of Arden—with the possible exception of the melancholic and cynical Jacques.

The philosopher, however, does not want merely to be *treated* as being of worth, he wants to question critically whether he *is* of worth; for philosophy is not concerned with opinions and values, but truth and worth. A kindly but deceiving acquaintance may praise my scribblings as art in order to make me feel good; but such flattery is a species of mockery, for if I am deluded into believing my feckless work is truly laudable, I am beguiled. Is not graciousness merely flattery? If I deserve reverence and honor, it is not by grace but by right that it be given; and if I do not deserve, to be given deceives. It would therefore seem a vice and not a virtue to be gracious. This is a serious critique that must be met honestly. Before we can ask whether we are of worth, it is first necessary to understand what being of worth means, just as we cannot ask whether we are truly grieved unless we know what it means to grieve. Yet, to know what grief means seems to entail being grieved, as Hume so profoundly points out. I cannot learn grief by the mere observation of another's grief—but this seems to put us in a vicious circle. To ask whether we are of worth is empty unless we know what being of worth is like, but if we already know what it means to be of worth because we know what it is like to be worthy, then the question of whether we are of worth seems begged. This is where the gracious breaks the circle, for in being treated graciously we learn what it means to be worthy even if the ascription of worth be undeserved. Learning what it means to be worthy by being treated graciously then makes possible our success or failure at it, for now we know what it means. We can, of course, learn what it is like to be worthy and not become worthy, but to learn what it is like to be worthy by being treated graciously at least makes being worthy a meaningful possibility. Being treated as worthy does not entail being worthy, but it does mean that being worthy is possible. Being gracious, as a species of this fine, thus opens the possibility of being worthy. Indeed, it is now possible to be worthy without being treated worthily, so the dependence of worth on being treated worthily is denied.

This is not a mere heuristic "priming of the pump," as if we treat graciously in order to get worth going, as it were, any more than the learning of grief by being grieved reduces the authenticity of this dread passion to morbid indoctrination. Grief is real even if the cause be false, as a mother's anguish at the false report of her son's death is no less potent than if the report were true. To treat graciously makes possible our grasp of what it means to be of worth even if, as in the mother's false belief in her son's death causing real grief, we fail at it. Her grief is not false; neither is our learning of what it means to be of worth false, though our failure to be worthy may render our learning merely conceptual rather than concrete.

Yet, even this analysis may be misleading, for it suggests that worth is entirely achieved, that it is the result of some laudable action on our part. If we can fail at being worthy, it seems possible that we can succeed, by dint of effort, to be worthy, and this reduces worth to the achievement of morally good conduct. But worth is a presupposition to the ascription of either censure or praise; we first must be able to be of worth before we can succeed or fail, so being able to be of worth is prior to, and not the result of, achieving moral goodness. It may seem that "being able to be of worth," which is inherent in our nature as agents, already makes us of worth, so that in effect we really cannot fail at being worthy, as is suggested above. But this critique fails. To be able to be rich does not make us rich any more than to be able to be good makes us good. There can be no doubt that our inherent ability to be good demands that we be treated as ends and not as means, and that certain civic and even moral "rights" can be claimed, rights that provide the opportunity to succeed and fail. However, nothing is sillier than the pseudoarguments that equate the right to be good with the achievement of it. Having the ability to be good may entail an inherent right not to be denied a certain respect, but that respect is not a guarantee that worth is equally found in those who have the mere ability to achieve it but do not.

There is a danger inherent in approaching this subtle but fundamental point solely from a mechanistic or speculative metaphysics. If worth is assigned not to being good but merely to being able to be good, and this ability is seen as a necessary presupposition for being human, so that all must have it inherently in their nature, the next step would seem to be to ask about the ability to be able to be good, and with this to begin the rapid descent down endless regress. If ability is taken as a sheer logical possibility, too little is said; but if by ability we mean a preexisting germ of a not merely possible but actual worth-entailing property, too much is being said. Such metaphysical speculation is entirely inadequate to the enormity of the problem since it adopts a mechanistic and causal paradigm of thinking. For the deeper, indeed, truer inquiry is not to ask what kind of entity we are or what kind of properties we possess that may account for our worth but rather to ask what it means to be of worth. Here, what "makes worth possible" is not some latent, preexisting property but a way of being and thinking that shows what it means to be worthy. This is concretely discoverable in the phenomenon of graciousness.

It may now be helpful to reflect briefly on the opposite of the gracious. If the gracious treats as worthy, the vulgar treats as unworthy. We must immediately note that the ungraciously vulgar is therefore not to be seen as necessarily immoral, for the vulgar need not deny any rights or inflict any wrongs, need not kill or rape or lie or cheat or abuse or mistreat. Rather, the vulgar simply does not recognize or treat as being worthy. There is, in vulgarity, an indifference to the fine, not necessarily a perpetration of immoral acts. This is why the classic vulgarian defense is always egalitarian: Who's to say it is better to dine off plates? Why not just put the food into your mouth as quickly and easily as possible? Who's to say good grammar and syntax matter as long as we are understood? Who's to say a belch is not as good as a "thank you" to show your appreciation of food? Who's to say the grunting lust of an animal is really all there is to the so-called refined, sacrificial love of Juliet for her Romeo? The vulgar refuses to see, or simply does not see the difference, and accordingly the notion of worth can play no role in making the difference, so worth is worthless. This, of course, is the ultimate reduction of vulgarity: the worthy are worthless. If the term *worth* has any meaning, this reduction shows the contradiction and hence irrationality of vulgarity; if the term has no meaning, nihilism follows. This is not to say that the vulgar are nihilists; it is to show that the inherent indifference in the vulgar to what is worthy, when pressed, leads to nihilism.

It is possible for the refined to be rude or vulgar as a means of willful insult, but in this case, it is the insult that matters; the rudeness is but the means to achieve it. In the more important usages, rudeness consists less of willful insult than of sustained insensitivity, a species of existential lack, more to be pitied than censured. For what is lacking in the mode of the vulgar is precisely the awareness that worth matters. To those born blind we owe a sympathy for their deprivation of the beauty in great painting, but not pity, for that insults. We do pity those with perfectly good eyesight who do not see the beauty in the painting though they may see the painting as an object within their visual field. The pity is for vision lacking, not vision denied. To be blind to worth is not due to a feeble mind but a feeble spirit, possibly left feeble by unrefinement or poor education. The vulgar, therefore, do not merely misprize the fine; in misprizing they diminish their own worth.

Vulgarity in this sense, however, always seems to bear with it an aggressive harshness, like a giant slob tramping on delicate flowers or a rude and rebellious teen popping the bubbles of pomposity among her staid and stuffy elders. However, this is misleading imagery, for the coarse slob destroying beauty is too easy a target, and pomposity almost always deserves its bubbles to be burst by the pinpricks of rebellion. There is always a danger that the refined be misrepresented as the stuffy and the clumsy be endeared by humor, which itself is possible only by refinement. Far more serious than these buffoons are the more insidious forms of vulgarity of which these stereotypes are but caricatures. The apelike insensate who tramples on the flowers is indeed coarse, and the image may help us see how truly disgusting it is to lack graciousness, but the ease with which he is dismissed may fog the broader landscape. If the essence of vulgarity is insensitivity to worth, which, when protracted, renders us without worth, it is not the grosser forms that deserve attention but the subtler, for in their very subtlety they are more insidious. The focus on these finer insults to the fine deserves an independent chapter.

Chapter 6

The Common

There is a paradox here. Elitist disdain for the common may itself be but a species of insensitivity, overlooking the deep but quiet loves, the unaired anguish and silent joys, even among those who live in oppressive suburban sameness. Perhaps it is even nobler to sequester in preciousness a wee spark of authenticity amid the drenching monsoon of the common than to flaunt a flame of elite refinement in the sunshine of the abundant. Yet, though there doubtless be mute and inglorious Miltons lurking in the dreary houses of the same, the same remains a depressing counter to the fine. When cloned by dull statistics to appalling frequency, even a sordid flicker of a petty but redeeming lust chokes out its own fire with fuliginous vapor. To approach a city's skirts in a jet plane, speeding over the sea of countless roofs like fig leaves hiding the shameful pettiness of the drones within, depresses. Humanity becomes a mass. But if beneath a few of these beetle roofs dwells nobility, as the odds demand, then what is this contempt but arrogant blindness?

What troubles here? Is it the sheer mass, as if in so great a multitude nothing remarkable can appear? Or is it the ignominy of statistics, the raw sacrilege of counting the great, putting on the few a dwarfing label of percentile? "Given any airborne vision of ten thousand houses, three percent contain dwellers of quality." The very suggestion gags, not because 97 percent may be dull but that to make it a matter of statistics insults all the way down to the aorta. Is there not indeed an ignobility in thinking about such things numerically? There is a fallacy, oft perpetrated by spoiled youngsters of some wit and less learning, that begins: "Most people believe that . . . but I believe otherwise . . ." placing the first belief on the lowest rung, as if sheer rarity of an opinion somehow graces it with rank and honor. Most people believe summer follows spring and only a few believe the silliness of phrenology or deconstruction; and in this the common have the truth and the few have the illusion. Perhaps the finest are entirely indifferent to such numbers; they care not whether their delight in Mozart is shared by all or none; why should it matter? The beauty is stunning even if no one else has sense enough to be stunned, and it is still stunning even if all are stunned.

Are the egalitarians correct in saying the great should not be praised since all are great? To deny that a great person can be born in a hovel is ridiculous since many great people were, from Christ to Beethoven. To say that in the cloned houses of the millions no great thoughts or passions can occur is likewise ridiculous. Yet, somehow, to say this great passion I am now feeling is merely what all the millions also feel every day, seems to deflate it into the vastness of the unremarkable. Must the great and the noble be actually, numerically rare? It seems almost logically necessary to say so, since universal greatness shared by all renders the term meaningless; yet the ensuing contempt for the common overlooks the hidden nobility in unfamed, countless struggles. If the gracious treats not only as worthy but as special, it would seem a most unsavory disdain for the vast throng of humanity must follow, and that itself is simply ungracious and unworthy. Yet, unless the graced be special and not ubiquitous, the very authority of the graciously worthy is lost. The paradox is not only real, it is painful.

Yet it is, and must remain, a paradox, not a contradiction. One meaning of the term *common*, when used as the object of contempt, is found in the more contemporary coinage *minimalist*—that is, barely achieving and being content with the minimal conditions for being human, according to which, the common are barely human. This does not mean they possess only the necessary properties to belong to the class whereas others possess further properties that adorn the class with finery; it means rather that the common think about themselves, if at all, only in terms of the lowest common denominator. They judge themselves with sheer minimal standards lest they be forced to achieve greater things by an effort and a risk they are unwilling to take. In this sense the term *common* indicates a way of thinking; and it may be a matter of contingent experience that the vast majority actually do think in this minimalist way. It is entirely defensible to chide those who are content with the common (i.e., minimalist humanity), for such contentment stifles both the achievement of and the appreciation for the fine. Under this rubric, the paradox seems eased, for it is not the censure of actual people but of an attitude of idle satisfaction and, hence, avoids elitist disdain for quiet courage among the many. But such easing deceives. Although it may be necessary to resist the tendencies of aristophobia within ourselves, the pathoempirical phenomenon of the actual vastness of the vulgar masses seems an essential element in a necessary disgust. Just as Kant argues that the sublime must be felt and not merely reasoned, in order for the pain and the glory of that experience to occur, so in the case of contempt for what is common there must be an actual experience at its base; and this experience seems to demand a revulsion at the sheer enormity of the bovine multitude we see around us. Even if we were to admit, duly or piously, that among the common are a few nascent Lincolns, the felt hugeness of the masses still repels, almost as an aesthetic revulsion.

How are we to understand this? Perhaps it is due simply to the difficulty in spotting a single person in a vast crowd, so that uniqueness is entirely absorbed in sameness, the way the pointillist's small blue and red dots are eclipsed into a vague purple when distance merges them. Or perhaps it is the difficulty in maintaining one's own ethical judgment when everyone else judges otherwise. Or perhaps it is the hopelessness of making any difference when billions else have not. Or perhaps it is the dreadful burden of truth itself, that so many of us are living lives of such staggering emptiness we feel we must entirely vacate the shared world but cannot. Or perhaps it is the fell realization of mob fever, that ugly reality when individually decent and even respectable people lose their sense of identity and react as a crowd, impelled by the basest of motives. We read about this phenomenon, and perhaps have even witnessed it; shameful participants in mass vulgarity later confess they felt their own personal responsibility and judgment slip away, replaced with a curious intoxicant of communal passion. This mutation of the one into a mindless many can be observed, can be felt, and can properly be censured as unfitting the nobility of the species.

In each of these possibilities, the abhorrence is *felt*, not merely classified by analysis or judged by critique but palpably endured, as a powerful, physical oppression. The logical possibility that each and every member of the mass or mob may also feel exactly the same sense of oppression is ratsbane in the food of truth. There are the common and they are base; and as vulgar they menace both truth and worth. As felt, this passion is either an empirical resource of useful information, or it is an aesthetic response, devoid of mere utility but precious as the basis of reflective judgment. To judge who we are seems to demand that we are not reducible to minimalist standards which are palpably repugnant in actual, gross majority.

There is moral danger in the elite disdain for the common. Every child molester defends his predation on the grounds that his victims actually consent. It is, they say, a mere common or vulgar view that children cannot, as the law insists, know what they are doing; hence, the common and the law are wrong and the molester is actually giving the child what he really wants. If false guilt were not imposed by the vulgar, the child would not be molested but simply pleasured, and pleasure is good. Biographies of many detestable villains follow the same plot: originally swayed to believe their unholy wants are wrong, the perpetrator nevertheless acts, finds himself feeling less guilty than he feared, concludes that the common censure against him is simply unfounded, and happily proceeds to ever-deeper corruption untroubled by guilt since he, being elite, dismisses the purely emotional judgment of staid and boring society. The appeal to license or elitist privilege leaves us unchecked by communal wisdom and censure, and depravity ensues. Curiously, the egalitarian protest that supposedly disarms the ethos of the elitist is made here on the elitist's behalf: who's to say my private little perversion is really wrong? Who am I to care what "they" say, anyway? Do we not rather need the common censure to keep us in check? The disdain has come full circle when the putative elite embraces the technique of the common to justify his own vulgarity.

These dangers not withstanding, mere adherence to the common seems unworthy. It is unworthy first because it relies solely on the minimalist understanding of who we are, and second because aesthetically the immersion into the vastness of the self-eclipsing multitude is repulsive: we turn our heads away from it in disgust. But these discoveries seem to suggest that the rejection of the common or vulgar is not really elitist at all. The term *elitist* has a pejorative ring to it, suggesting arrogant contempt and a lack of respect for other people. The term seems to connote a private club of spoiled bigots looking down on the less fortunate, unconcerned about their wretchedness and misery. Lack of concern for others has already been shown to be a quality of the vulgar, not the fine. To treat another without grace or a sense of worth is what it means to be common; those who are gracious are not elitist at all; they are rather noble. In the vernacular, even this term is sometimes equated with elitist disdain, but such equation itself is merely an extension of the already suspect vulgarity of disregard for fine differences. The fine contempt for the common is not for individual people but for the masses as vulgar. The magnitude of their number, rather than inspiring wonder as in the experience of the sublime, inspires revulsion just because, as vast, it absorbs all uniqueness, as a wide bog swallows the unwary, leaving a quivering, stinking, undifferentiated scum covering all its swallowed victims.

The rejection of the masses by the refined is supported by two distinct pillars: (1) the aesthetic revulsion of sameness, and (2) the moral refusal to judge ourselves by minimalist standards. The countering rejection of elitism is also based on two pillars: (1) the unanchoring of moral restraint, and (2) the insensate blindness to noble struggles among the common people. These opposing pairs of moral and aesthetic sentiments constitute an inescapable paradox since without contempt for the common the fine itself is impossible, but with contempt for the common the fine seems indicted by a species of vulgarity—which is, to treat without regard for worth or truth. By refining terms we see that this opposition is not self-contradictory, but no amount of clarification can defang the anguish of the paradox entirely, for the revulsion against the common is palpable and real, just as the arrogant insensitivity to the courageous struggles by common folk is itself vulgar and likewise palpable and real. Those who dwell solely within the ranks of the common need not feel the anguish of this paradox, for they can dismiss all refinement merely as corrupt elitism; but those for whom refinement matters must not only accept the anguish but also actually embrace it, for the anguish is essential for the fine. Perhaps, then, the most fundamental distinction between the common as vulgar and the few as refined lies precisely in this painful embrace of the paradox. We think of the noble not merely as superior but, in their superiority, sacrificial and courageous. These terms deserve reflection. From its etymology, sacrifice means to make holy; and from its usage it means to yield what is dear for the sake of the precious. Courage, as Plato shows us in the *Laches*, does not mean to be without fear, but to confront fear without loss of worth. So the noble yield the dear to make possible the precious, thereby establishing the holy, even as they confront, in this making-possible, the fearsome, without loss of their own worth.

But this makes nobility itself paradoxical in its essence, for in yielding what is dear it is unattractive, even as, in making possible the precious, it becomes sacred. The common, if seen as contrasting the noble, in its defense of what is dear, frustrates or impedes the possibility of the precious, and, hence, is unholy or profane. The modality of the common is therefore entirely unparadoxical, for it is of the untroubled and tranquil.

In chapter 5 it was shown that the vulgar are indifferent to worth and truth. To this is now added the discovery that the common, as vulgar, are entirely untroubled by the paradox of the few as fine, namely, that as being fine, they make possible the ranking of the precious over the dear. Vulgarity thereby reveals itself as a species of idleness or even laziness, an unwillingness to confront truth and worth simply out of a resistance to what disturbs in such notions. The vulgar are simplistic; the fine, simple; the former prefer solutions, the latter endure the troubling. But the common has great power to satisfy—to make dear—and thus cannot be discarded.

The phenomena of the fine arts manifest the possibility of embracing both sides of the paradox. The truly great artists, such as Verdi in his operas, Shakespeare in his plays, and Mozart in his music, manage the embrace without losing its tension. Even the street urchins of Milan were quick to pick up on Verdi's enormously satisfying arias, singing them lustfully in the streets within hours of the premier performance. The plays of Shakespeare were and are attended by fairly unsophisticated audiences who revel in their power to evoke strong emotions; and Mozart's music soothes even the most savage beast. Yet Verdi's refined treatment of both character and counterpoint evokes respect and even stunned admiration from the musically and dramatically erudite, the most critical of literary critics finds wonder in Shakespeare, and musicologists spend lifetimes in reverent analysis of Mozart's concerti. How are we to understand this? One way we should not understand it is cynically, arguing that these great creators sought to please the crowd with the more emotional aspects of their art, thereby ensuring financial success through the broader marketing appeal; and at the same time sought to please the critics by the more cerebral refinements of subtle craftmanship, thereby ensuring fame and recognition among the elite. This cynical account misses the very thrust of true greatness, which pleases simply even as it refines nobly. One no more can divide the loveliness of Mozart's denuding melody from the intricacy of his treatment than one can surgically remove the flame of carnality from a revering, gentle love. Indeed, it is the reverential, awesome adulation by the deeply erotic lover that, in banking the fires of his or her lust, whitens the heat to a searing intensity. The exaggerated respect shown the beloved is not distinct from venereal passion but a refinement of it.

Art can therefore sabotage its own refinement by the embrace of its conceptual elements only, dismissing the palpable as too common; it can also be sabotaged by yielding to the allure of the merely emotional in contemptuous disregard of refined craftmanship. There is something narrowly elitist in purely conceptual art, especially if it is self-indulgently obscurist—indeed, it becomes almost prissy in its artificial delicacy, eschewing all emotional joy for cerebral satisfaction in the solving of puzzles or for the bookish tickle in identifying shadowy causes and influence, as if art had footnotes more relevant than the text. This sin against art is more serious than its opposite—that of relying solely upon the most immediate of visceral responses—for the latter lasts only hours or weeks and has no pretensions, whereas the former, sanctioned by academic approval, is placed into the deep freeze of vaunted scholarship where it long outlasts its original claim to cleverness. Music written merely to challenge the musicologist, painting produced to puzzle the critics, and literature written to send scholars on forays into the obscure are all elitist in this negative sense; popular art that appeals solely to the most vivid of visceral delight, which is either shock for its own sake or raw, venereal allure, is vulgar in the most offensive sense. Yet, great art cannot dismiss either entirely, which is why such art is always alive with unresolved tension. This brief appeal to artistic synthesis by the world's great masters is not meant as a contribution to criticism or appreciation—though it may provide such illumination—but to vivify just what "being common" means, and why nobility cannot be equated with elitism.

This incursion into critical aesthetics focuses attention on the noble's paradoxical relation to the common. It is a paradox because the fine cannot merely dismiss the common as the elitist does, yet must retain a felt revulsion at the vulgar as common. If we discover that the fine sacrifices the dear for the sake of the precious, we must now make our thinking more precise on such matters.

What is dear is what is needed to be happy or at least content, hence, of huge importance, possibly incapable of being outranked; or if it is to be outranked, nothing within the realm of ordinary thinking could achieve it. What is precious is that which ennobles and awes us by its mere presence, making us greater and smaller at once. We may justifiably endure pain and loss in order to achieve or protect what is dear, but only the precious can be the ground—though not the justification—for sacrifice. The deprivations endured for the sake of what is dear are in the order of cost—that is, a price we are willing to pay in a prudential calculus in order to achieve what is desired. Those deprivations endured for the sequestration of the precious are not payments but offerings, the way a gift becomes a sacrifice when the giving is painful and the bestowal is made out of reverence rather than in expectation of a more valued benefit. The noble are judged as sacrificial, not because generosity is a virtue but because sacrifice alone sequesters the precious, giving it a sacred precinct set aside from the common traffic of the everyday. The dear and the precious are therefore rivals, and in the mode of the ordinary, the dear must matter more and must come first; for only if the dear already matter can they be offered up or sacrificed for the sake of the precious. Ardently the common latch onto the dear and cannot, as common, admit their sacrifice; the noble perforce cannot disdain the dear else to yield them would not be sacrificial. Since we can only sacrifice what is already dear, and to disdain the dear is to render them undear, it is cruelly necessary to suffer their loss if sacrifice is to be made possible. It is this cruel necessity that the elite as well as the vulgar are unwilling to accept. The disdain by the noble for the common is therefore not for what is dear, but for the unwillingness to sacrifice; and this disdain is necessarily palpable (i.e., felt), for suffering, which is essential for sacrifice, cannot merely be only thought but felt. If we must feel the pain in order to sacrifice, we must also feel the disdain for those unwilling to sacrifice. Such feeling is not a mere empirical resource for information, it is aesthetic and, hence, reflexive.

The sacrifice of what is dear for the sequestration of the precious reflects the second of the two qualities necessary for the noble as fine: courage. If courage is not the absence of fear but the confrontation of it without eclipse of our own worth, we now see how this belongs to our understanding of nobility. For if we ask for the *sake* of the painful endurance in courage, we recognize that not just anything we value will suffice. There may well be a species of nonnoble courage in the common willingness to endure the loss of one benefit for the sake of a greater benefit; but in order for courage to be noble, it must not only endure a loss but sacrifice what is dear for the sake of sequestration. Noble courage is remarkable precisely because as sacrificial it endures the pain of confronting the fearsome without loss of worth and establishes a new and sacred precinct that alone makes the loss of what is dear meaningful. This precinct is the precious, and sequestration is of its essence. Just as a child finds a secret garden, nook, or niche in which she hides her treasures and thereby bestows upon that special, nonreplaceable, and precious spot the aura of wonder and even holiness, so the noble as noble sequesters from the hungry eyes of the everyday that consumes its treasures, the precious, that as hidden is not used up but kept as sacred.

The common, therefore, in their defense of what is dear as beneficial to them as a source of need and happiness, constitute a threat to the very ability of the noble to sequester what is precious, and must be rejected with contempt, for what is rejected is the very insensitivity to the autonomous worth of the precious. Yet, since in order for there to be such a thing as the precious—in the sense of sequestered holiness—there must first be sacrifice, and since what is sacrificed must be dear—else the pain necessary for sacrifice would be lacking—this contempt cannot forfeit the very essence of the common as holding dear. We must first hold dear before we can sacrifice what is dear.

We cannot turn this around. The common cannot sacrifice the precious for the sake of the dear, for there is nothing in the precious that matters to the common, nothing that would bring suffering in having to yield it. Only the dear can be sacrificed for the precious since sacrifice itself is essential for our courageous confrontation of the fearsome that ennobles by the confrontation. The common can, and often do, yield one dear thing for the sake of a dearer thing as a kind of payment, and insofar as this payment may entail a form of pain or suffering, it may be a kind of courage. If the endurance of suffering must be accomplished without a loss of one's own worth, this possibility seems somewhat remote, for what is gained by such suffering is not an ennobling of our worth but merely the acquisition of greater benefit. We may call such suffering minimally courageous if, in the exchange of what is dear for what is dearer, no loss of one's worth takes place; and whereas such is surely possible, it would seem that any reflection on this endurance of pain as itself worthwhile would entail some sense of the precious and not merely what is dear. A boy having to endure a painful therapy to save his limb may be willing to yield what is dear (avoiding pain) for what is dearer (saving his limb). It is difficult not to imagine that such endurance also changes who the boy is by ennobling him, and such ennoblement would be precious rather than dear, and the ensuing suffering would then be sacrificial rather than merely of cost-value. In the sacrifice of the dear for the precious, we shift from what is of *value to* us, to that which enhances the *worth of* us.

The vulgar, in essence, treats without worth and values without truth. The elite, though uncommon, are therefore vulgar; but the noble, as sacrificial and courageous, treat as worthy and esteem as true. It is impossible to be noble without disdain for vulgarity and even commonness, yet at the same time esteem the worth of the individual, common person. This internal paradox creates a painful tension within the fine, a pain the vulgar refuse to accept. If the fine as noble must revere truth itself, it now becomes necessary to explore what it means for the fine to treat the truth itself as precious.

Chapter 7

Fine Truth

Solecisms in both behavior and language offend the sensibilities of the fine. It hurts the lover of language to hear "he don't play no good," and it hurts the lover of etiquette to see a diner chew with his mouth open and wipe his nose on the sleeve of his dinner jacket. What offends is not so much the impropriety of the actions themselves, but vulgarity for its own sake, a fatty indolence threatening the health of the culture like cholesterol hardening the social arteries. It is the obesity as well as the ubiquity of the unhealthy that offends. The sheer deadweight of the insensate threatens to smother the life of the fine.

There is, similarly, a deadweight obesity to philodoxy, that species of vulgarity that loves opinion rather than truth and that threatens a far nobler concern than mere etiquette or grammar. What concerns here is not the falseness or invalidity of academic relativism but the deeper threat of vulgar indifference to truth; and, hence, by a kind of disjunctive syllogism, it matters that concern for truth rather than belief be seen as refinement—that being fine requires truth mattering—just as being vulgar requires that truth not matter. Although it is already made clear in this quest that the fine concerns both worth and truth, the recent reflections have focused more on the gracious treatment of worth, with truth seemingly appended as a caboose to earlier trains. But the quest has now reached alpine heights, and in the rarer air the climb itself digs more deeply into the lungs for breath. What has the fine to do with truth?

This is not to ask whether or how the fine knows more than the vulgar, for that need not be assumed. Nor does it ask specifically about the nature of truth, though indirectly this may come into play.

It certainly does not suggest that the truth is only about the fine, since we may know as true many vulgar facts. It does raise the question of the nobility of truth mattering and the baseness of indifference to it.

It seems at first mere tolerance. Familiarity with past disappointments in our beliefs makes us chary of dismissing claims counter to our own. Unwilling to adopt an unjustified certitude, we tolerate diversion of opinion in the hope that from this we can extract newer and more enlightening views and hence continue to learn. True tolerance is therefore in service of truth. Yet it seems so facile to place the machine above the work it does and rank tolerance as an end in itself, as if it were a virtue to suspend the worth of truth and play only with its tools. To claim something as true now seems a hindrance to overly promoted tolerance, the way the police, originally designed to serve the laws, so easily become a police state and, hence, laws unto themselves. What follows is not true tolerance but intolerant sport, in the double sense of mocking and playing. The game played is one in which all players are equal, so the sporting goes on without victory, without rules, and without end. There may be a kind of delight in such aimless playing, as cleverness may delight at the cost of profundity, but it is, upon reflection, profoundly vulgar.

This deserves an unusually deep penetration. Why is philodoxy vulgar? Perhaps it may be wiser to invert the question and ask, why does vulgarity, when unchecked, lead to philodoxy? To understand these questions as questions, which is necessary before any response to them can be given, the nature of the allure inherent in philodoxy must be exposed. For the love of opinion is still a love, and must be understood as such. What attracts in philodoxy is not, as one might expect, the epistemic open-mindedness of the critically cautious, as certain methodological skeptics seem to offer, nor the resistance to dogmatism apparently offered by the relativists, but the fun, comfort, and false importance offered by membership in the philodoxic community. Being a love, philodoxy is diametrically opposed to the skeptic's bitterness, for the latter rejects all and the former embraces all. The skeptic denies any claim is worthy of our adherence, the philodoxist affirms all claims as worthy of our adherence. That these two extremes may conflate into a common misology at the end does not relieve us of understanding their differences. Similarly, though the philodoxist may be reduced in the end to the relativist's feckless paralysis, the lure of the latter rests on a grim, puritanical theory of truth as unobtainable certainty, the lure of the former is quite other. The nature of its lure, enticing a thinker to the genuine evils of skepticism and relativism, must therefore be exposed since, unlike them, the danger lies in the very attraction.

To love opinion, after all, is to delight in the very activity of the speaking animal—not that what we speak need always be true, for that seems outrageous and false—but that speaking itself offers us a playground for delicious games. This metaphor of gaming is carefully chosen, for playing is always both at once entertaining and, as entertaining, unserious. It is precisely because opinions are not anchored to the truth but find their support in private, personal utterances, that they seem to make us, as their originators, important. If what I say must be true, then it is only the truth of it that matters and not my saying it; and, hence, my own personal significance seems diminished. Because I need not defend opinions, I can curiously recognize that adherence only to my own is not necessary, indeed, may be myopic. I discover that the wanton profligacy of opinions, mine as well as others, provides a community of unlabored glee simply in their abundance. There is a playfulness inherent in this, and an entirely unexpected boon of communal camaraderie, the nature of which is both comforting and corrupting.

What is the latest idea floating about? We run to it, embrace it with all the fervor of the new baptized, disdaining the heady intoxication of last week's idolatry as passé. We chatter among ourselves, trying out the delicious new syllables of the tagged opinion, finding in our new faith a kinship with the other converts. As the gaggle grows, new sprouts of thought spring up, bolder, daring, exciting, fun. There is a special kind of bonding that consists precisely of this sharing of the urge to give mouth and voice to opinions in their infancy. But is it rational? If not, let us change the very canons of reason to accommodate it; for after all, if the newness is what matters, a new logic is better than an old. The old logic is but a chain impeding our freedom. To opine the new is to become unfettered. This is heady stuff, and not for the loner; it needs a togetherness, as drinkers seek out their own kind, for only as shared intoxicants can the blurring be enjoyed. The great fear is to be left out, to be thought yesterday's advocate, the lowest form of life, the traditionalist, bound by the ossified, tired old beliefs that hang like tatters of disgrace on the withered shoulders of the senile. Join with us in the giddy hot tub of the new nakedness, unashamed now of our prurient privacy only recently discarded, a bacchanalia of unrestricted, common sharing, like venereal orgies of wanton promiscuity. There is fun in this, a gorging of forbidden fruit that must never become separated from the throng lest the nakedness show. This is the new age, the revolution, the felt union with the thrust of history, scorning all who are left behind.

But wait. All the panting, sweating, heaving multitude throbbing with the pulse of the new . . . over there, on the far side of the playground . . . can it be? A newer one? Why were we so eager for the first new? It is the second new that is newer yet. Hurry. Run as fast as you can, over there, where a younger, fresher opinion glitters like a virgin waiting to be deflowered. Yes, we agree, just now we were painting with a new color and the pigment is not yet even dry, but who wants what is dry, arid, set, congealed? But what *is* this yet newer opinion over in the corner where even now the bonded friends are unbound, bounding like rabbits? What a tired and dreary question! Who cares what the opinion is, that it is new is all that matters. Is it, though, really new? Let the fusty old scholars worry about that—it is new to us, gleeful in our belonging to the latest trend.

So they bounce from new to new like a shuttlecock, buffeted by the racquets of disdain for what is scarce old enough to span the smallest gap of time, and the leer of the newest pusher with the latest pills and the promise of the higher high. That these are gaggles of geese seems not to matter. What matters is not being left behind, for that is the deepest fear. How dare you speak of truth—for that binds—opinions are free. They make us free. We were all Feuerbachians. We were all Marxists. We were all new wave. We were all deconstructionists, post-postmodernists, post-post-post-neo-modernists. The labels matter absolutely, for nothing else can. They identify us, make us one. Perhaps not like a bacchanalian revelry, for that too passes. No, it is more like . . . well, yes . . . like a religion. Quieter, more respectful of our inner selves, at one with the universe. We'll play Gregorian chants, shave our heads, try out the new chastity. Ah, there's nothing like a religion to bring us together. It is the communal that matters now, the camaraderie, the common.

Philodoxy is by its nature wanton, for opinions are numberless. To love opinion is to seek refuge in what is believed. Believed by whom? By those most ready to believe, most ready to accept simply because acceptance is expected and common, and, hence, by those least ready to think or reason. But if reasoning itself becomes a fad, it too can be believed, as long as it serves to excite the crowd, as it obviously can. Reason as carnival is as old as Plato's *Euthydemus*, as recent as dialectical thinking, which accepts the absurd as surd, as new as tomorrow. Reason itself, unanchored from truth, can support opinions and, hence, propagate the love for opinions, philodoxy. This makes the foolish into the silly; and though we all are fools, we need not be silly, for the silly are vulgar. Folly can be made reverent in great comedy, as Shakespeare endears us to the fools in *Midsummer Night's Dream*, but the silly cannot be revered by any magic, even the poet's. To be silly is to toss from wave to wave in the surf of belief, and this communal thirst for distraction rather than truth is entirely silly and entirely vulgar. There is nothing fine in this froth at all.

But the allures are still there. To reiterate: philodoxy is loved because (1) my opinions are mine in a way that truth is not mine, so opinions seem to make me matter; (2) precisely because there can be many opinions but only one truth, philodoxy offers camaraderie; and (3) the sport of hopping on the latest fad is simply fun. Like the Sirens calling Odysseus, these lures threaten to bring us to the dashing shoals of a peculiarly base form of folly, silliness, and to guard against their fake charms we must bind ourselves to the mast of truth. The first of these charms is guile, for although opinions may be uniquely ours in a way truth cannot be, the necessary equality of opinions renders them equally the same in importance, and so, that we matter in our opinions turns out to be vacuous. Our opinions do make us important if and only if they are candidates for truth, but such candidacy changes the precinct from philodoxy to philosophy. It is only because truth matters that we can matter, so the importance offered by opinion is sham importance, hence, vulgar and deceitful. The second charm, camaraderie, is also sham, for what is offered is the transient distraction of mere acquaintance rather than the true and rarer phenomenon of friendship. A false friend is precisely that shadow of a friend who relies on the mere froth of fleeting interests shared merely because of their brief prominence. Again we are beguiled, for true friendship matters just because it outlasts the passing moment of the fickle crowd, whereas the fragility of papered proximities comes apart in the first rain. The third charm is the most challenging of all, for who can defeat the appeal of fun? Fun based upon our delight at our own folly is truth-bestowing; fun based on silliness is really self-mockery rather than self-amusement. For even the glory of fun, made sacred in great comedy, requires truth in its denuding, else true fun is beguiled merely by contempt, where the laughter is hollow, the glee cruel, and the amusement base.

Philodoxy thus reveals itself in this depiction as vulgar and crass, turning its advocates into pathetic and silly geese at whom we can only laugh in contempt, not with whom we can laugh fondly. That such silliness can find near-manic advocacy in the noblest institution, the academy, where truth alone should rule is pathetically sad; but it shows the power of the lure. That the silliness of philodoxy is not a mere solecism, however, but genuine barbarism, can be seen in the political consequences of philodoxy raised to the level of power. For when truth is replaced with opinion by the weavers of argument, and the thinker becomes the opinionater, ideology, which always and only succeeds through terror, replaces statecraft, and millions are ravaged. This is silliness wed to power, and the effects are ghastly. For terrorism is nothing else but the collapse of authority. The silly become the dangerous. When fun is misplaced and put into the seat of power, it becomes tyranny.

Fun, camaraderie, and importance—these are the lures of philodoxy. All three do matter, for their lack invites grimness, loneliness, and worthlessness. But the essence of the silly is usurpation, placing the pretender upon the throne. The lures turn out to be forgeries, for though they tempt with the promise of fun, they provide the grim; tempt with camaraderie, but offer abandonment; tempt with importance, but render triviality. These deceits are crass. We find true fun, friendship, and importance not in the vulgar delights of opinion but in the refined nobility of truth.

Vulgarity, in order to be vulgar, must quarantine truth just as it quarantines worth, for there is a self-indulgence in being common that forfeits any nonarbitrary standards. There is a sad paradox for those seeking to trumpet their own importance by the brassy voices of the arbitrary; for in order to succeed it must render the multitude as its guarantor, relying not on truth but on a majority—indeed, a majority not freely determined but terrorized into unanimity like cattle herded by the raucous barking of dogs.

This unseemly debauchery contrasts vividly with the love of truth, in which, transcending the fickleness and terrorism of the arbitrary, a certain dignity can be anchored. The fine are not swayed by every passing wind, for though they may well err, such straying is capable of being checked; and as a consequence rather than merely tossing from one belief to another, the errors become painful but steady progress of authentic learning. It is this solidity that gives the fine the noble bearing afforded only by the reverence for truth. The fine esteem themselves precisely because they are not buffoons; rather they find dignity because as truth-lovers they are anchored in the reliable, exactly as the honorable are trusted but the political who offer empty promises are not. We find an order amid chaos; and when the times swell darkly with what is fearsome, such order is salutary.

Yet, as formidable as such constancy is, and as important as it is to our understanding of the fine, to seek anchorage in itself is not enough. For philodoxy loves opinion as such and, hence, becomes giddy; but orthodoxy—the claim to right belief—offers a bulwark against this silliness, and yet falls short of nobility. To replace the love of all opinions with the love of one opinion deeply believed may offer the hope of anchorage without reverence for truth. Those who deeply believe their opinions do so because they hold them to be true—in this they are a step above the philodoxist, but as mere orthodoxists, they as yet remain wedded to belief and not to truth. This may seem a merely formal distinction, since caring for true beliefs seems but minimally distinct, if distinct at all, from caring for truth, for what else is true except beliefs or propositions that can be believed? Yet this difference, though subtle, is anything but merely formal, and certainly not minimalist—if understood, it may be of the most critical importance, for what constitutes fine nobility is the difference between the love of a specific true belief and the love of truth itself.

Even if the deeply held belief actually be true, to esteem it is not to esteem truth, for what matters in holding it deeply is the putative rightness or accuracy of its claims; but what matters in esteeming truth is the possibility of learning. In the strictest sense, only truth is learned, for to learn the false is really to mislearn—though we can and do learn from our errors and mistakes—but more significantly, truth is learned rather than known. To argue in this way is admittedly to fly in the face of the revealed religion of the epistemologists. Hence, some care must be taken to justify this rebellion, and to distinguish, if you will, the lovers of knowledge—highly esteemed as these may be—from the lovers of truth.

According to the lovers of knowledge, a true belief, however deeply held, as yet does not constitute knowledge, for such true belief must as well be supported by justifications or arguments. This view, that knowledge is justified true belief, can be found as early as Plato's suggested definition in the *Theaetetus*—knowledge is true belief plus *logos*. In recent years it has been highly refined by the challenges from Edmund Gettier as to how we ought to understand the justifications. Knowledge surpasses mere opinion, celebrated by the philodoxist, and even true opinion, claimed by the orthodoxist, precisely because in addition to the mere true belief, the knower must have rational or otherwise justified support for maintaining the belief. This seems to hedge against the tendency of the orthodoxist to adopt intolerant or dogmatic resistance to counterclaims by allowing reason to play a critical and hence publicly open role. It seems obvious we would not claim to have knowledge if our belief were true merely by fortuity or luck—that one who merely guesses correctly that 1066 was the year of the Norman conquest lacks knowledge even though the answer is correct. Thus, since knowledge by definition requires openly testable support, it not only outranks orthodoxy, it also introduces the critical and supportive qualifications and, hence, is a kind of reflective refinement.

There is nothing to quarrel about in this. Knowledge is admittedly distinct from mere true opinion on the basis of evidentiary or critical support, and hence it is finer to know the truth than simply to believe what is true. It is logically odd to say we know what is false, so the very fact of knowing also bears with it the truth of what we know, so the knower knows what is true. It would seem then that the esteem for knowledge as the corral of truth must also esteem truth for its own sake and thus be the most noble of all states. How then is it possible to suggest that it is not knowledge but learning that is of the highest rank? This seems even more dubious when it is pointed out that the dictionary defines learning as "the acquisition of knowledge," making it appear as a mere means in service of the more fundamental treasure, knowing. If to learn that Chicago is south of Minneapolis gives me geographical knowledge, then learning is entirely dependent on the possession of knowledge and has no intrinsic worth or status. Commonly understood, the definition is correct, and the subservience of learning to knowledge is obvious.

Part of what troubles is that, so conceived, knowledge is always after the fact; it is something already known when analyzed. We speak, perforce, about "states," such as being in the state of knowledge or in the state of ignorance, or of "propositions," embodied independent of our learning them, or even of "facts" that are known as characteristics of the world independent of our having to know them. Knowledge is always knowledge-that, so that *what* is known is always a proposition. There is great epistemic precision in thinking about knowledge this way; indeed, it may even be correct. But if so, then the mere possession of knowledge cannot be the finest state. To know that St. Louis is south of Minneapolis is now an item in my consciousness, conceived always first as a proposition, then a belief, which then turns out, because it is knowledge, to be true. But this makes knowledge dependent on truth, not the other way around; and it freezes the development of learning into time frames, as if we pushed the pause button on the video recorder, disjoining one image from its predecessor and its follower. How I learned of the higher latitude of Minneapolis, what follows from knowing this, indeed, even what it means seem all to be locked out of this propositional time freeze, treated as a completed event, now over but recalled. I feel a draft upon my neck and turn to discover why. The window is open. Voilà! I now have knowledge. The proposition "the window is open," is true prior to and independent of my believing that the window is open. A proposition is either true or false, and is true rather than false if and only if it corresponds to what is the case. A belief is true or false; and true only if it corresponds to the proposition; so there are two correspondences, one between the belief and the proposition, the other between the proposition and what is the case. The latter correspondence gives us truth, the former, knowledge. How I "come to know," (i.e., how I come to possess the belief as an item in my mind and then link it somehow to the true proposition) is called "learning." But this priority of the proposition seems to leave out what is most important: the actual linking up the belief with the proposition and then linking the proposition with what is the case. Simply to label it "learning" and then to define learning in terms of knowing seems backward or even circular. There is no reason why we cannot reverse the project defining knowledge as that which has been learned, rather than learning as the acquisition of knowledge.

But learning happens, it is not a state, belief, proposition, or disembodied image being looked at by the mind. Because learning happens, and knowledge has happened, and thus is now a state, belief, proposition, or image, the priority may be reversed. There is, however, no purely formal way to determine the preference between defining learning in terms of acquired knowledge or knowledge in terms of what is learned; the preference can be revealed only by asking about what it means for truth to matter.

The notion of truth revealed in the analysis of knowledge need not matter at all, for I know trivial things and profound things equally well; I can know without knowing what knowledge means, and the number of things I know is so vast as to be incomprehensible. The most vulgar, feebleminded wretch may know as many things as a nobel prizewinner, and though what the laureate knows may be more important than what the wretch knows, such importance is entirely irrelevant to its being known. The streetwise pimp knows many things the saintly provider of solace does not, all of which by definition are true. So truth as that which is understood solely as a necessary condition for knowledge does not seem to matter very much, since both the trivial and the momentous are alike in being known. In this sense it cannot even be said that knowledge has utilitarian benefit, for I can know things that bring me grief, I can know things I ought not to know, and I can know things that were better left unknown. Yet I can, in being ignorant of some things or believing in some false opinions, become a far greater person, a morally better person, and certainly a happier person. It is simply false to claim that to know is always more beneficial than not to know. That we may nevertheless rank knowledge above ignorance cannot be due merely to the nature of knowledge as justified true belief. Indeed, the ranking may be false; what matters is not that knowledge is always better than ignorance—for that is false—but that truth matters independent of the consequences of knowledge.

Learning, however, is always of importance, especially if we realize that the mere acquisition of knowledge is not a sufficient account of what it means to learn. What we learn is the truth of our reality in the sense of becoming who we are. This is possible only through refinement. Just as perception can be refined (as noted in chapter 1), we now realize that who we are can also be refined, and this refinement is called learning. But what we learn as refinement of who we are is always and only truth itself, for it is logically perverse to say we learn what is false. We can, to be sure, be misled by false teaching, and such mislearning can be corruptive or satisfying but not true. We can be led to believe falsely what we assume to be true, but this would not be to learn. We can also be led to believe true propositions about the world, such as that St. Louis is south of Minneapolis, and this may be called a kind of learning, but only in a minimalist sense. Ordinary language supports such usage, and it would be churlish to deny the authority of accepted, ordinary convention; but we are not perforce required to limit our understanding of learning to these common conventions.

If to learn is to refine who we are and what we learn is truth, then truth must be fine, in the sense of being achieved through refinement of who we are. The refinement of perception, already established, is now revealed as a kind of learning in which what we learn is truth. Unlike knowledge, which must be a state, learning is an event, unfolding in the process of refinement and therefore something that happens, that is, a phenomenon. Even if we insist on the everyday expression that learning is "coming to know," what compels our attention is not the state of knowing but the act of becoming.

We speak, for example, of learning or not learning from such resources as history or our own mistakes. Thus, it is possible to know the facts that led the Northern commanders to defeat at Chancellorsville but not to learn from them; that is, what it means to let the smaller force out-maneuver the larger. Our knowledge that we make mistakes, and even our more precise knowledge of just what our mistakes are, does not entail that we have learned from our mistakes and, hence, learning cannot be reduced merely to the acquisition of knowledge. To speak of learning in this broader way seems to consist in part of going from propositional "knowledge-that" to an understanding of what it means and, therefore, a refinement of our being; that is, we learn by refining who we are becoming to be. To learn is to refine our reality. The metaphor here is perhaps that of the guild, in which mastery welcomes the apprentice through the disciplined refining of those skills that changes him from a novice to an expert. This guild is existence itself, in which what is learned is to be fine.

The point here is not to establish a thesis about how we learn to become ourselves—an exciting endeavor on its own—but merely to show that truth, as learned, is refinement. But there is much that is troubling in this. For one thing, just as knowledge seems capable of analysis only after the fact, learning seems to depend on futurity, which necessarily must remain unknown though not unthinkable. We learn only as we unfold into what we are becoming, and, hence, strictly there can be no "acquisition" at all; to learn attests to our finitude and incompleteness. This does not regress to the earlier giddiness of philodoxy, for truth unlike opinion is not arbitrary or even pluralistic; but neither is it fixed as in orthodoxy or even fixed and rationally supported as in knowledge. As futural, learning-based truth beckons, and the lure is our own becoming fine. It is naive optimism to assume that truth promises some inevitable success, as if, were we to practice hard enough, we could assume we would eventually play in Carnegie Hall. The struggle to achieve mastery may be thwarted by a simple lack of talent or even the eclipse of all success by misfortune, as when the would-be pianist loses his or her fingers in an explosion. We do not even find redemption in the worth of the struggle itself, though there is certainly more to be commended in this than in the starry-eyed assurance of success. These assurances are but promptings against despair, if not the false bromides of promised success were the effort but sustained. But if success is not the lure to truth-based learning, how are we to think of it?

That there be truth in our refining who we are, rather than guaranteeing success, quite to the contrary, reveals the possibility of unsuccess. Vulgarity refuses to recognize the difference—that is, it accepts success and unsuccess equally—and knowledge refuses to recognize ignorance. Since learning is futural, it must be ignorant in some sense, for we do not know the future nor are we in complete control of our destinies. So there is no guarantee. However, there is truth, and not merely accomplishment, in learning. In becoming who we are, learning must always be of truth. In this sense, then, truth is refinement; and indeed to unfold our own truth is to be fine not vulgar. The reason we can say this is because truth is now no longer a mere characteristic of certain propositions but of being itself. In becoming fine we become true: this is the deepest sense of learning.

Watching Bottom the Weaver make an ass of himself before the Fairy Queen reveals the deeper mysteries of our own being foolish; our laughter at his folly endears us not only to Bottom, who after all is a mere character in a play, but also to our own reality as inherently foolish. To witness Leonora's courage and loyalty in *Fidelio* mirrors our own respect for or participation in the matrimonial sacrament of fidelity made radiant by Beethoven's music; and Michelangelo's Sistine Chapel reveals, as architecture and fresco, what it means to worship. Our cultural sacraments therefore reflect ourselves, not as we are but as we would be refined to be. This is not some goal exterior to the artistic phenomenon but truth lurking within it. The study of Newton's notebooks or even the challenging mathematics of Einstein's theory of relativity also refine our confrontation with the physical world and, thereby, enrich us. The unfortunate overemphasis of the distinction between the arts and the sciences can only thwart our grasp of what true learning is, for mathematics and science, if conceived as cultural sacraments, ennoble as do the fine and liberal arts. Our passion for taxonomy requires we appreciate their differences, but our greater, truth-generated passion for synthesis requires we embrace them all as our own.

There is another educational distinction that, if overstressed, threatens the integrity of learning as refining our becoming, and this is the necessary though dangerous difference between teaching as providing knowledge and educating as extracting thinking. Defendants of this distinction often point to the episode of the slave-boy in Plato's *Meno* to show the superiority of extractive techniques. As a consequence they belittle the role of teaching in the narrower sense, depicting it as a dreary drone of rote in which mindless pupils memorize the oft-repeated reiterations of traditional lore or the baleful tedium of swallowing unchewed morsels of information that lie undigested in the stomach until regurgitated at test time. There are obviously uninspired wretches behind desks that still do this today, though their offerings are all the more offensive for being sociopablum; but this unkindly fact should not indict the practice of teaching by instruction. It is just as offensive to shelve the books of greatness and substitute them with the putative "Socratic method" as it is merely to recite memorized slogans or bits of information, indifferent to their refining of the learner. It is not the difference that matters here but their wedding, as male and female become newly one in the sacrament. In one very important sense the distinction breaks down entirely. To offer to the uninitiated the towering grandeur of Sophocles' Theban plays must perforce require instruction—they must be forced to read, hear, and preferably witness something entirely new to them, without the insipid persuasion that such drama merely reflects what they already know, as if the agonies of Antigone can be reduced to their petty squirming with suburban frustrations. If these plays are presented as awesome and wonderful, the learner finds an echo, not in what she has experienced or even reflected on prior to confronting the dramas, but on newly uncovered dimensions of her own reality that now trouble her with entirely unfamiliar yet still self-mirroring passion. Why deny them such magnificence? The absurdity of stressing education as extractive over teaching as instruction is embodied in the ridiculous adage "let them think for themselves!" First, thinking is the one thing that cannot be done for or by themselves since thinking is rule governed and, hence, universal. So the maxim should be shortened and made far more elegant as "let them think!" Second, by emphasizing the need for *approval* by the student, the regress to philodoxy is almost irresistible.

The wedding of instructive showing and educational extraction avoids the vacuity of both extremes but also forges an entirely distinct phenomenon alone worthy of the sobriquet "true learning." What can be extracted from the untrained is at best the purely formal inferences of connection, either logical or mathematical; what can be forced by rote becomes mere recognition made acceptable by familiarity; and even to conjoin these is merely to test what is familiar by the canons of rigorous coherence. When the receiving spirit of the learner welcomes the lamp that probes into his interior darkness simply because of the joy it provides as truth, what is extracted is not what is already known but an eagerness to a self-discovery that, as discovery, amplifies and changes what is discovered: our own becoming; and what is provided by instruction is not mere information made familiar by rote but new mirrors that allow for the discovery to occur. This phenomenon can only be understood as a new refinement and a shunning of old vulgarity. Terms such as *knowledge* and *propositions* cannot explain this phenomenon, nor can the mere techniques of extraction and instruction. From the glorified anguish of Antigone's torment, the suburban youth can find no parallel in his own experience, which seems dull and vulgar by comparison; but as the learning of the drama unfolds, he embraces this ennobling of his own soul, which was not his but now is, and the joyous welcome of it surpasses the language of communication or epistemology. He was always fated to some extent, but the confrontation with Oedipus reveals what it means to be fated, and in this he is refined. This refinement alters the way he reflects upon his own reality. From the fun and camaraderie of philodoxy, he develops a joyous welcome of noble sharing. Why these terms? Why "joyous welcome"? This cannot mean that learning always makes us happy; for since what we learn is truth, the bitter as well as the delectable must be embraced. Learning need not bring joy at each lesson, rather it makes joy possible just because it embraces truth. The genealogical development can be here resketched in four steps to show how learning welcomes.

1. In philodoxy, glee is taken in artificial self-importance and camaraderie. Glee is delight taken in play, which as play need not revere truth. Art as a form of profound play does indeed reveal truth, but then it no longer provokes mere glee, which by definition is always distinct from what is appreciated.
2. In orthodoxy, glee is replaced with a sturdier and more reliable satisfaction in what is constant. There may also be a certain self-satisfaction in superiority over the infidel.
3. This is then replaced by the love of knowledge, which delights in the assurance provided by justification; a sense of superiority accompanies this due to the role that critical reasoning plays in the support of knowledge claims.
4. This is surpassed by learning, in which the glee of the philodoxist is replaced with the joy of truth, the steadiness of the orthodoxist is replaced with the refining of the learner, and the assurance of the knower is replaced by the welcome of the lesson. Joy is not happiness, nor is it glee. Essential for joy is triumph, and what is overcome or defeated is the wretchedness of the lower states as forms of vulgarity, not by removing such ignorance—for that is possible only in the blindness of orthodoxy—but by transcending it, the way a lover rejoices in his capacity to endure suffering because it allows for ennobling sacrifice for the sake of the beloved. The joy in learning is not to be found in what we learn, for we may learn what is dreadful, but in the triumph over what is vulgar in our innocence. Learning allows our miseries and misfortunes to be ennobled by the tragic, which the vulgar cannot accept, for tragedy as a reflected or mirrored art form refines our suffering into self-denuding and, hence, truth that none of the prior stages can endure.

If this is so, then not only is our learning of truth to be understood as a refinement of who we are becoming, but truth itself must be fine. For the fine is also the radiant, beckoning with the lure of welcome as it stuns with unaccustomed brilliance, even as truth must do if it be capable of being loved. This point is subtle in its profundity and deserves the independent chapter that follows. For the great danger here is fantastic utopianism, as if truth were somehow transcendent of earthly existence made unreachable by mere mortals—the territory of gods. But truth is earthly, the stuff of humans even if it be fine. This itself needs refinement.

Chapter 8

Transformation

"Among the glaciers and the rocks," the poet Auden tells us, "wakes the hermit's carnal ecstasy." This is a stunning image that probes deeply into the mystery of human love, but its power to stun lies in the conjunction of the unexpected. Are hermits carnal? We tend to think of them seeking isolation in the desert to shun the flesh, not embrace it. They eat locusts and wild honey to deny the thrall of taste; divest themselves of fine clothes to answer with their nakedness the sharp whip of storm and fiery lash of sun. They exile human welcome altogether to purify themselves of the common. This perverse celibacy of all the passions, like that of eunuchs, nuns, and old men who have forgotten, seems antipodal to carnality. Yet the poet places among the rocks and glaciers an ecstacy of this passion. Why? Perhaps in his desert nakedness there is the evocation of the very lust he would cover. Fierce hunger is a sauce for all banquets. In struggling to harness the fiend does not the hermit unleash a far more feral beast? Perhaps there is none so carnal as the hermit. We seem to wreak deeper bondage whenever our efforts to be free assume titanic proportions, so that ecstasy may nowhere be so starkly felt as in the wretched, pitiful loneliness of this misguided, cadaverous figure in the desert. He is surely more racked than the bawd, the pimp, and the whore, and on the rack he howls unwittingly the very heresy that put him there. Has the hermit not divided too severely his flesh from his soul?

In the quest for the fine we cannot forget the origins, yet neither can we simply return to them. Philosophers make distinctions to avoid conceptual clashes, but if we find satisfaction in the mere fragments that lie cut off from each other like shards on the floor of the mind, we have purchased consistency at the price of coherence. For we distinguish to avoid inconsistency, the way we distinguish body from mind, lest the necessity found in logic be equated with the contingency found in experience; I am not two beings but one, and if we cannot think and feel together, we lose the coherence of our primal unity. What we sever with a distinction must be healed with synthesis. To distinguish the fine from the vulgar is necessary to climb; but, like the misled anchorite, we cannot pretend gravity any more than lust is conquered, lest in believing so it conquers us. We distinguish the fine from the vulgar; but if we oppose them as opposites and not somehow bring them together, the distinction no more enlightens than ghetto walls that divorce the affluent from the desperate unify a city. For the hermit's attempt to divest himself from the lustful simply renders him, at first glance anyway, grotesquely carnal rather than pure, and the fine becomes vulgar. Yet, the hermit's wrestling with the common urgencies of the flesh remains uncommon, and unenviably magnificent. He cannot be dismissed.

The poetic image of the hermit's ecstasy is not merely a warning that lust denied becomes lust triumphant, though that may be the secular reading. Nor is it simply the magnitude of his struggle that we can admire without emulation for his courage. The image also tells us that the hermit has found in divine intimacy a passion more fiery than the burning of lust, that because he is an erotic, aching, finite being, the confrontation of the infinite is not cerebral but passionate. In this image the hermit is less a perverse distortion of healthy lust than a lofty, momentous transformation of visceral urgency to the rapture of sanctity; he is not a hollow-eyed victim of frustrated yearning for denied flesh, but simply a saint. In this image, the saint is revealed as far closer to us sinners than we may want him to be. Thus, the carnal hermit troubles us in two ways: we fear to sublimate too fiercely the vulgar passions, lest they turn against us in a savagery of self-eclipse; and we fear that in the titanic struggle we may be forced to confront the dread possibilities of our own latent, possible sanctity, a horror far more draconian than the first.

The fine, therefore, cannot divorce itself from the vulgarity of its innocence or its origins; it rather transforms it as suffering is transformed by the glory of sacrifice or folly is transformed by the genius of comedy. The elite disdains the common and therefore becomes vulgar, but the fine transforms it. The failed hermit simply finds deeper bondage to the flesh, whereas the holy hermit transforms his lust to rapture. Yet, is it this simple? Is not the risk of failing ever present even to the saintly hermit? Is not the desire to transform also present in that lonely, failed hermit as well? There is the terrible risk in hermitage. Perhaps indeed the final, emerging saint first passed through the shame of carnal bondage exacerbated by the desert, reaching rapture only through the dreadful passage of self-mockery. There is no simple solution; the risks are there in either case. If there is an analogy here, it is that the fine must transform the vulgar, not disown it; and that to make the trek of transformation is highly risky. Not to make it is to rest content with our base origin, a contentment bought at the price of self-respect.

How are we to transform, and how is it to be understood? It is already shown that the transformation is a kind of learning rather than knowing, so that the fine beckons as truth. But now, it seems, this learning must be seen as a risky transformation; the authority of the origins cannot be dismissed, though neither can they satisfy. It is for this reason that we speak of the vulgarity of innocence, for in the distortion of nostalgia lies an existential fallacy. Innocent children are sweet, precious, and lovable; their observed innocence often wrenches us with retrograde aching to return to it ourselves, or even to halt by some fantastic dystopia the child's achievement of the putatively cynical and jaded maturity toward which she seems to rocket with unholy speed. Yet, no decent parent in spite of these undeniable feelings thwarts her child's natural growth, and no authentic adult is entirely misled into the adoption of warmed-over innocence. Yet, things are not as simple as that. The charm of innocence is not entirely dismissable; or rather, it can be dismissed but only as fallaciously as to submit entirely to it. For innocence gives us, in its confrontation, something of considerable worth; it is neither a simple ignorance of good and evil, nor a warm womblike refuge into which we can retreat nostalgically. For being an adult does not necessarily entail jaded ennui and cynical dispassion, though there are those who, forgetting the worth of original innocence, find in their maturing an isolation from fervent youth. Innocence transformed is not knowledge but wonder. Without wonder, philosophy itself cannot occur.

It is a mistake to see in simple childhood fascination true wonder; for children are not in awe of what they see, they merely delight in the playful novelty of experience. Adult observation of this delight, however, evokes a respect for the ability to see freshly all that is about them, and the very company of children often teaches us to see things as if we were seeing them anew. Mere feigning of unfamiliarity is deceit, for we are not newcomers to the world as is the child. It is precisely because the child is unfamiliar that there can be no true wonder. To imitate childlike delight is therefore disingenuous, for it is based upon pretense. We cannot seriously pretend that the rims of color rounding a soap bubble promise a new experience, as it does to the child, nor can we be amazed that these diaphanous globes explode or vanish at a mere touch, for we already know bubbles pop, and it would be a cheap deceit to pretend that it is amazing that they do. But reflected—not original—innocence can become a resource for true wonder, in which our finite but expanding awe teaches us the only truth whose worth needs no purposive benefit: the meaning of our own becoming who we are.

The newness of experience is often a conceit. The first hearing of Beethoven's *Hammerklavier* is rarely as moving as subsequent ones, if for no other reason than its sheer complexity thwarts ready appreciation; the first reading of Spenser's *Faerie Queene* may be tedious to the student but awes the sophisticated reader. There is a misperception that first encounters are always more genuine and definitely more awesome; but except for bee stings and shrapnel wounds and other unexpectedly intense invasions, the first experience of most events distracts precisely because of its newness, especially in the arts and in human intimacy. It is not the new but the renewed that stuns to true wonder.

To transform innocence is therefore not to retreat to some preexperiential naiveté, which as naive is simply incapable of wonder, but to submit to the adventure of a world richer in its renewals than in our memories. "Oh, what authority gives/Existence its surprise?" Auden asks in "The Sea and the Mirror"; and there is no doubt that the authority he seeks is art, always a reflection of experience, not the simple experience itself. But why should this be thought as a "reformulated innocence"? First, such innocence is not naiveté, for what we are innocent of is not the event but what the event means; it is yet a kind of innocence precisely because it is not repetitive or guilty, that is, its realization is neither a simple recurrence that custom makes stale, nor a burden of regret from which we turn away in moral revulsion.

Our original vulgarity, as origin, is forgotten only at the expense of meaning; the quest for the fine cannot abandon this origin entirely nor can it be allowed to impede renewal. What gives existence its surprise is not a barrage of entirely unfamiliar experiences unlike in kind any we have known before, but the revisitation of the original in a surprising and surpassing way, as learning sensitizes our appreciation, rendering the old world new. Specifically, the vulgar as vulgar is revisited in the comedic art, which, in mirroring our own folly through the expanding prism of aesthetic fondness, celebrates our finite origins without being a mere slave to it. In the same way, suffering, itself a vulgarity, is transformed by noble self-learning into sacrifice, which is fine. What is meant by the fine is, therefore, not the antivulgar but the vulgar transformed.

If Auden is right and art is the authority that gives existence its surprise, and if the only truth learned that is worthy in itself is the meaning of our own becoming who we are, it is obvious that refinement cannot gainsay our vulgar origins nor turn away from the learning that ennobles. Only in this way can the hermit's denial of his flesh be seen as inviting greater sexual bondage, even as his struggle with it renews it and thereby renders it spectacular making the very carnality itself holy. What we learn finely is truth, the truth of our becoming who we are, discovered by means of the authority provided by art. Each of the terms involved in this account, that is, authority, surprise, truth, transformation, and becoming who we are, deserves special, indeed, reverential accounting.

Authority compels through legitimacy. If I first falsely believe that to affirm the consequent is to affirm the antecedent, this error can be pointed out to me by an appeal to the legitimacy of my own reasoning; so the knowledge that if there is abuse there will be scars does not validate the inference that scars indicate abuse. The validity of my critical reasoning is established by the legitimacy of how I think, and thus to learn by my own reflection on logical validity is authoritative. Though I may disapprove of his policies, I do not deny the right of the president to call out troops since, as duly elected, there is legitimacy to his authority. The president may be unwise in his call to arms, and disaster may follow; the scars may indeed be the result of abuse, though my realization of this cannot be achieved through false inference. In both cases, I am compelled by legitimacy alone to assent, and by this is meant that to deny either the authority of presidents or of my own reason is to submit only to external force, which forfeits my worth as a rational or civil being. Yielding to unworthy probings such as the simple forces of fear or indolence, usurps my integrity. I may still be rational or civil in some sense but would lack any worth in *being* either.

In a similar way art has authority. It does not merely please the senses but reveals who we are in a way that compels assent, for as Heidegger so ably argues in the "Origin of the Art-work," what happens in the confrontation of art is truth itself, and truth, no less than reason, is a legitimacy that grounds the authority to compel assent. Through Shakespeare's genius, the folly of Touchstone's vulgarity—"Sluttishness may come hereafter!"—becomes a revealing mirror of our own originary vulgarity now raised, through this artistic confrontation, to the level of the fine. It is not the vulgarity of Touchstone that matters, but the enforced confrontation of our own removed folly by the authority of great art. This is the "authority" Auden speaks of, that gives existence its surprise.

Surprise is violence to expectation. What is expected in the case of our existence is not, as may first seem, the familiar, but rather a curious form of unfamiliarity, namely the numbing exile of being unaware, which, as exile, keeps us from the familial or familiar. In the drone of this exile, what surprises is the suddenness of return. Art is the authority that surprises by the unexpected welcome found in the home from which in our idleness we had strayed, and had unknowingly reentered through what we thought was just another door. To say art surprises suggests that to be artless is to be common or vulgar in the sense of jaded exile; what stuns is the return home, where the welcome, having been forgotten in the sojourn, reasserts its authority on us as dwellers. We are expecting beings, and what we expect is, almost by definition, the unsurprising, for it is logically odd to be surprised by what we expect. As unsurprising, existence is common. The unexpected, however, is not the arrival of some entirely novel or foreign agency, but the opening of the welcome door where we belong, for commonness or vulgarity is a mode of unbelonging and, in this exile, unsurprised. Touchstone's bawdy witticisms surprise us precisely because they are familiar, the way Mozart's perfect largos surprise us with deep familiarity, making the familiar new. We are surprised, in other words, because it is ourselves discovered in the finely wrought mirror of the vulgar Touchstone.

If surprise is violence wreaked on expectation, the nature of the violence itself must be understood. For mirroring to occur, a certain degree of harsh severity is needed to rip ourselves from ourselves; for if we are the ones being mirrored and we are also the ones looking at the mirror, a cruel self-severing must take place. The violation of common expectation is always harsh, though there may be joy or at least delight in it, but as harsh, there is a painful jolt as we suffer a division of ourselves into seer and seen. There is a violence even in authority based on legitimacy; but when this authority is that of self-discovery mirrored in art, the violence is to homeless expectation, and it thrills rather than terrorizes, though it may yet wound. Self-severing—that is, dividing ourselves into seers and seen at once—may wound or thrill or even do both, but its nature must always consist of being torn away from the comfortable expectation of being without being seen, which is to be in a state of unsurprised commonness or vulgarity. The error here, which must be resisted, is that truth-bestowing surprise removes us from our home-based belonging and compels us to venture to alien lands; in fact, it is the other way around: truth-bestowing surprise welcomes us back to our belonging and, as violent, pulls us out of the distraction of being a tourist where we forget who we are.

Truth that has its worth intrinsically, and not purposively, can only be found in this painful or at least stunning surprise of self-disjoining in which what it means to become who we are happens as a phenomenon. Knowledge is useful and hugely beneficial; and the possession of knowledge may even please us simply by having it; but truth inherent in self-learning alone is of worth rather than of value, for in facing ourselves, we become ourselves. To be who we are is to become who we are becoming; for as finite, we are always becoming. What matters is not *that* we become, for such becoming is simply inherent in our temporal nature, but *what* we become—that is, our transformed selves. That this truth of our own self-becoming matters is the essence of the fine; and vulgarity, though it can never be entirely discarded as origin, consists of indifference to this truth.

Self-revealing truth happens. It is not a relation, nor is it a state or belief as knowledge is. To say truth happens emphasizes the transient unfolding of our meaning, which if it matters, is refinement.

Transformation from vulgar origins to refined self-revealing is therefore based on the authority of truth that compels assent through the legitimacy of becoming who we are. If we characterize this transformation as refinement or as becoming fine, we now recognize something of extreme importance that, up to this moment in our quest, has only been a shadow in our reflections but now deserves to be brought under the light. The fine is authoritative. This is to say that the fine compels rather than merely offers, and such compulsion rests on legitimacy. To transform or to refine is thus more than a mere possibility and even more than a mere option; it has the authority to lead us to our truth, which, as legitimacy, is reliable and needful. The proper realm of the fine is revealed, therefore, as not merely in aesthetics or ethics or even metaphysics, but in existence: it is an existential truth. The transformation of the vulgar to the fine bestows authority on our own becoming. We do not simply become, as if we cannot fail at it the way we cannot fail at growing older; nor can we become whatever we want, as if modes of existence were items on an ontological menu to be selected as entrees in a restaurant. Authority, however, is not necessity; to say existence transformed becomes existence with authority is not to say we are determined, beyond the altering reach of will, to become one way rather than another. It is to say that the fine, in transforming vulgar innocence to noble wisdom, leads, as generals lead troops or as conductors lead orchestras: a leadership that wins battles even against uneven odds or brings music out of noise. The authority in the fine rests on the legitimacy of truth.

The distinction between the fine and the vulgar does not constitute a mere taxonomy of classes, for once the authority of the fine is realized, it becomes clear that the revisitation of origins legitimizes; and, hence, unrevisited or untransformed innocence is illegitimate, in which illegitimacy is a species of untruth precisely because it lacks authority.

"Becoming who we are" may seem a strange candidate for the ontological ground of that which is transformed and whose truth alone is of intrinsic worth. It surely cannot mean that we are like seedlings inevitably becoming full-grown plants. The developing participle "becoming" is linked to the more constant phrase "who we are" in a way that forfeits either extreme: we are not constant entities whose change is understood merely as the addition or subtraction of properties; but neither are we mere processes in which the flux of change alters so radically that mere waiting achieves a different reality altogether. The phrase "becoming who we are" identifies our reality as capable of refinement, but not necessarily: we can become who we are not, in the sense of regressing from the fine to the vulgar; or we can fail to become by assuming such a deep vulgarity that sameness entirely chokes off all learning. In this sense, the phrase refers not to an entity but to an ontological ground of meaning, which is what should be meant by the term *reality*.

The phrase, therefore, suggests our reality is itself a story. We often speak this way in ordinary discourse, as when we identify our lives as stories, equating the "life" of King John with the "story" of King John. We often ask "who is she?" in a way that invites a response, "She is becoming a leading candidate for mayor"; and even when she is elected, the same question prompts a reply, "she is becoming one of the best mayors in our history" or even "she is a mayor who will be remembered." This identity of who we are with our own becoming need not suggest any fatalism or determinism or inevitability, nor does it imply a teleological metaphysics, as if each of us has a specific telos or purpose that, if we achieve we are worthy of our existence but if we fail we are unworthy of our existence. It is far simpler yet far deeper than these metaphysical explanations. To speak of our reality is to speak of the ground of meaning, the way the reality of a constitution gives meaning to the social and civic truths of a state, or even the reality of a desk gives meaning to the various kinds of things we can say about it. To suggest, as the phrase in question does, that our reality (who we are) is to be refined or vulgarized (becoming), renders an account of our reality precisely in terms of the ways in which we are able to be thought about—that is, ways in which we are meaningful. To suggest we can fail at becoming who we are through vulgarity and succeed at becoming who we are through refinement gives an ontological basis to the notion of the fine.

It is, after all, possible to seek our reality in the sense that who (not "what") we are is something at which we can succeed or fail. Since we do not usually know what our own becoming portends, it is almost irrelevant whether such destiny is in some mysterious, metaphysical way already written in the stars or whether its discovery and even its reality awaits the unfolding of our story in which we play a partially determining role by our own will and strength or weakness of character. Such speculative accounts, being equally possible, and in themselves offering nothing to inspire trust one way or the other, returns the speculative metaphysician to the giddiness of philodoxy, and is thus unworthy of thought.

Chapter 9

The Wretched

To make precise by contrast—a philosophical method necessary for an existential inquiry such as this—admits the danger that what is to be made precise—in this case, the fine—may have multiple counterimages; and to focus only on one distorts by selective myopia. We may, for example, seek to clarify our understanding of hope by contrasting it with despair, using a careful and rich analysis of those abandoned in this miserable state to throw light on what it means to hope. However, unless the thinker realizes that presumption, in which hope is entirely forfeited because of assumed certainty of success, also contrasts with virtue, the ensuing analysis will not only suffer from incompleteness but may mislead entirely by identifying hope with unrealistic optimism, leaving us more beguiled than before we began the inquiry. In this present attempt to understand the fine, various contrasts have already been made of three different kinds of opposition. The fine has been contrasted with the common, which was rejected because of its minimalist appreciation of who we are; it has been contrasted with the crass because of the aesthetic revulsion inherent in what this reveals about who we are; and it has been contrasted with the vulgar in its various guises, which found satisfaction in the unrefined perception of who we are. As helpful as these approaches may be, however, they do not exhaust what it means to contrast the fine, and, hence, they as yet do not complete our precise understanding of it. This lack may be fulfilled by a careful consideration of yet another, and final, contrast.

"Wretched Queen, adieu," the dying Hamlet says to his murdered mother in the final scene of Shakespeare's play. Why does he call her "wretched"? The supremely gifted poet does not fail, ever, in his selection of the perfect, revealing term. The prince does not call Laertes or Claudius or even himself, wretched, though they all are also dead or dying. They may yet still be wretched, of course, but the dramatist reserves that term for the fallen queen, and the sensitive audience hears in the word a revelation. Why is she so depicted? Perhaps by briefly examing her fate and character it is possible to understand better the use of this remarkable term.

A good director has a certain problem in deciding how to instruct the actress who plays queen Gertrude, a problem that lies in one's interpretation of the play, namely, what is the degree of her guilt? Is she a coconspirator with Claudius in the murder of her husband? Is she entirely innocent? To assume she plotted with her lover to assassinate the king is to view her as thoroughly wicked and lacking any right to our compassion. Yet, if she is totally innocent, she becomes a mere victim, and indeed a fairly stupid one, whose death becomes merely pitiful. Yet, Shakespeare seems deliberately to avoid giving sufficient textual evidence to make her position absolutely clear, though he is not remiss in showing her character. She is certainly not stupid, for she possesses obvious political cunning and Claudius himself relies on her for advice. Just as certainly she is not entirely innocent, for the contrived play "The Murder of Gonzago" afflicts her as well as the king. This manifestation of guilt may possibly be due to her merely having betrayed her first husband with her adultery, yet it seems to go more deeply than that. The dramatist's unwillingness to tell us outright exactly her degree of guilt itself is a marvelous use of his craft to show us how she may think of herself. It is most likely that she too is uncertain but has growing suspicion of Claudius's chicanery. Yet because she is in the giddy, middle-aged, adolescent state of being in love, she resists the evidence but cannot escape the subpoena it warrants. Hers is a sanguine personality; she loves life, she loves men, and she loves being queen, all likeable qualities; but the delight she takes in her new rapture can only be sustained by self-deceit. Hamlet from the beginning is aghast that she would turn from the reverential and respectful love of her first husband to the mere rakish, passionate unbridled love of the younger Claudius. But this merely tells us that Hamlet does not understand his own mother's sexual urgency. When he visits her in her chamber, it is not merely the unseemly carnality that he evokes to persuade her to seek redemption, but the ominous suggestion of her being an accessory after the fact to regicide. This abetting of murder is so tightly woven to her self-deceit that the whole play turns on it. Carnal rapture, especially among the middle aged, can deceive even to the point of self-induced blindness to criminality. Gertrude's anguish at being forced by her son's accusation to confront herself reflects Hamlet's own twin agonies: his inability to act on the command of the ghost, and his own genuine passion for Ophelia. For, although he truly loves her, he sees in this love the same rapturous enslavement that corrupts his mother. Is this what rapture brings? A defilement of one's own judgment? So the prince lashes out cruelly at his beloved Ophelia, punishing her as a woman, as a substitute for Gertrude. The queen, rapt in her youthful passion, seems able to sustain her self-deception until the very end when she sees with horror that the drink is poisoned. The revelation is brutally cruel, for in this fierce moment of denuding she sees three dreadful truths at once: her husband is a murderer; she has deceived herself guiltily; and her son is in mortal jeopardy. She tries in her last agony to warn him, but it is too late. As Gloucester is a mirror to Lear, so Gertrude is a mirror to her son. They are both tragic figures: she deceives herself because of a beguiling love and hesitates to confront the truth, and he deludes himself into uncharacteristic impotence because of a beguiling reverence against sacrilege, and hesitates to act. But Hamlet has a redemptive experience in his confrontation with Fortinbras's army; Gertrude learns too late and can only wail briefly. He is nobly tragic; she is wretchedly tragic.

These brief reflections suggest that she is identified by her son as wretched in part because she disgraces herself. She may well have been ignorant of Claudius's villainy, but it was a sequestered, guilty ignorance; she should have known. Yet, caught in the vortex of her fate, she was all the more miserable for her self-deceit. The wretched cannot extricate themselves from the chains they have forged. This is why the indictment of wretchedness is so troubling, for the wretched do seem to be victims of a cruel fate they cannot control, but they themselves are the origins of that fate. So there is pity for the wretched as there might be for the simply miserable or unfortunate; yet there is also censure, for the miseries are self-induced. These two sentiments are in conflict, since we should not censure those who are pitiable nor pity those who deserve censure.

The wretched Gertrude is more than a model of pity vying with censure, however. The etymology of the term suggests the wretched are those exiled from where they belong; they are literally wrenched or wrought from their homes. They are in the cruel paradox of not belonging where they belong. To say the homeless are wretched is redundant, for to be wretched is to be homeless. Claudius is a clear usurper; he does not belong on his brother's throne, but the queen does; yet in uniting with the usurper, she, too, seems not to belong. *Hamlet* is more a family tragedy than a political one; Gertrude's blatant self-deception disfamilies the family, and so her wretchedness, as a form of exile from where she belongs, is self-induced. In a similar vein, when Claudius, in act 3, laments his own inability to pray, he identifies his state as "wretched" precisely because in order to ask forgiveness he must surrender the effects of the sin, and his will is not equal to the task. His prayer is not to be forgiven, but to be able to pray that he can be forgiven. He is wretched because his incapacity to pray is due to his own character.

The great significance of these deeper meanings to the term lies precisely in this, that wretchedness is not fundamentally a moral term nor is it a mere depiction of miserable conditions. It transcends the limitations of either realm of discourse; indeed, it vexes both, for it seems to make untenable the strong, exclusive disjunction between them. The wretched seem incapable of extricating themselves from their doom, but this very incapability, which normally would bar censure, is of their own making. For there even to be such a thing as wretchedness, therefore, embarrasses the moral metaphysician who would censure only willful acts and only pity the miserable. The wretched are caught between these two realms of discourse, so that the very phenomenon of wretchedness reveals that these two realms do not exhaust the ranges of our existence and our thinking. For those who are wretched, the suffering lies in the realization that they can find no solace in either guilt or misery. To the morally guilty, relief can be found in restitution, punishment, and forgiveness. To the miserable, solace can be found in the realization that the suffering is undeserved, and, thus, there is hope for both justice and sympathy without eclipse of one's moral worth. The wretched, however, are denied both of these extrications.

This is a formidable realization, for the distinction between culpable and inculpable now no longer seems exhaustively disjunctive. Moral ascription has always admitted of mitigation, but the wretched are not eased by mitigation; on the contrary, their censure seems curiously all the more intense for being wedded to their character or fate. The nature of this censure itself is singular, for what is indicted here is not our acts but what we have become (which is not to deny that what we do in part makes us who we are). It is not the unfair censure of blaming us for actions we cannot avoid, since it does not accuse us merely of what we do but of who we have become. Just as we forgive precisely because who we are is not exhausted by what we do, so we indict as wretched not those who merely do bad things but those who have become victims of their own degradation or enslavement. That the language and prescriptive range of morality is here transcended is troubling, not because such transcendence in any way weakens the universality or authority of morality, which it cannot do, but because to admit the possibility of such transcendence makes us dreadfully vulnerable and lonely. The phrase "beyond morality" is often seen as dangerous because of license, as if we somehow could appeal to special privileges allowing us to escape the stern prescriptions of duty and their consequences of guilt and responsibility. In this context the phrase is horribly opposite: it suggests a realm of censure unprotected by the stable authority of moral reasoning, a realm that is wretched, in part, because it seems inescapable and oddly deserved.

It is worthy of note that Hamlet's dying and final appeal to his mother echoes the same term the ghost of his father used to haunt his son: the French "Adieu!" Not an English word, it suggests the very homelessness and aching of exile; but it is also a transcendent appeal to the divine, "to God" etymologically, bidding us to enter into the realm not of good and bad but of forgiving welcome and wretched abandonment, where fated character weighs more than proper actions. Wretchedness seems, therefore, to offer the very concrete possibility of failing to become who we are; and if it be possible to fail at it, it would seem necessary that we can also succeed at it. So, by the technique of achieving precision through contrast, we gain a new sense of what it means to be fine: to triumph over what makes us wretched, to reach who we are in essence. However, our reflections show that this cannot be seen as a mere prescription, as if we could "avoid" becoming wretched and "achieve" refinement, in the same way we ought to avoid breaking promises and to achieve compassion. There is an element of such prescription, to be sure; but its meaning is not reducible to admonitions of behavior. We speak here of refining and corrupting ourselves, and, hence, the realm of discourse is existential rather than moral or descriptive.

There is a metaphoric use of the term *wretched* when applied to inanimate objects in the expostulation of disgust at their failure to function properly. "These wretched weapons" means they do not suffice; they are inadequate for the job; the enemy has superior technology rendering our defenses worthless. There may lurk behind these protests indictments of the government for the indolence or folly that left us so poorly armed, but the immediacy of the disgust is with ineptitude or failure to live up to what the weapon is designed to achieve. This usage, though indirect, is helpful; for we see that the queen is wretched precisely because she does not live up to what we expect queens to be. Rather than by her presence holding the state together, she erodes authority, and the Norwegian foreigner Fortinbras takes over Danish rule. Even when the object is fairly mundane, as when we say "this wretched lawn mower," we express a kind of minor outrage at sheer uselessness or shoddiness, for the frustration is with the lack of purpose.

When the scissors break, the lightbulb burns out, or the car battery cracks in the cold, we throw them out; they are worthless. This complete rejection of the wretched among the inanimate is a mirror to human wretchedness, where what fails is not purpose—since we are not merely means for the sake of something else, even God—but rather our own nonpurposive worth or essential meaning. It is also possible to "feel" wretched without deserving to be judged so, and this phenomenon further reveals how we think about being wretched, even if it is felt without warrant.

He was a mature and experienced thinker, satisfied with his work and position; he seemed to embody the Aristotelian account of happiness found in contemplation, free from enslaving sentiments, not putting his heart on things that rely on the fickle favors of others. A growing friendship gives him an unfamiliar satisfaction. He is surprised to find an unexpected shock of joy whenever he meets the friend, and after some time of familiar yet ever novel wranglings in his heart, realizes the friend is beloved. He abandons his earlier satisfaction in independence, and delights instead in the very dependence on his need, joyously willing to prostrate, if he could without embarrassment, before his beloved friend. His earlier independence seems cold and fishlike compared to the warmth of this new affluence of sentiment; and he takes no little joy in the realization that the friend seems also to share the delight in the speciality of their companionship. But these halcyon days are short; he notes the friend grows more polite than eager, respectful rather than spirited. A gap widens, and like a festering wound, discolors with doubt. Few things agonize as deeply as to watch a precious friendship unravel strand by strand, weave by weave. He senses that his own anxious desperation, if manifested, would be an accelerant to the dissolution, and so a pitiful, painful game of pretense wallpapers over the widening cracks. It is like going through a turnstile in which the blocking bar does not yield as we rush into its resistance, which punches painfully into the stomach, whoofing the breath out in an ache of wrenching. Yet, there is no antidote to this bane of eclipsing worth, for the joy that now fades so rapidly was never his by right but only by bestowal. Indeed, it was its very gratuity that so flattered and even honored him. Unable to make any moral redress, confused, and further vexed by his confusion into clumsy incompetence, he watches with impotent horror the sad unknitting of the glorious fabric of affection. He is rejected in the offering of himself; the ultimate preciousness of his own reality is mocked by stern, polite, icy disinterest. Neither, however, can he exculpate himself; for though no deed of his was at fault, whatever it is about his character that first charmed now repels; and his own being, rather than external circumstances of miserable fortuity, is the basis of his loss. So he indicts himself, not his actions, which are faultless. He is wretched.

To be rejected because of who one is cannot offer any solace. When Cain offered sacrifice, which is always a vicar of oneself, it was rejected, and not just by anyone, but by God. Had the sacrifice merely been insufficient, Cain would gladly have offered more. Sacrifices are gifts that represent who we are, and when they are rejected, so are we. Little wonder that Cain was so disgruntled and outraged, for nothing hurts as deeply as rejection of one's own self. There is always solace in our moral reserve; beleaguered by huge misfortune, we can at least remind ourselves that we have acted properly, that our moral worth matters even if our practical or personal enterprises misfire. Or, shattered by misfortune, we can take strength and comfort in the resolve to duty and moral conduct. To promise better behavior in the future often sustains us when losses mount, and the reason for this is that the autonomy of moral worth offers us a reliable anchor strong enough to weather unsettling storms. When this moral anchorage is irrelevant, when our reliance is not on merit but on bestowal, the loss of it is devastating, for it is our own reality that is spurned, not merely those actions that we can alter. Yet, because it is our own, neither can we avoid responsibility. We have lost the friendship, and so we bear the shame of the loss. Protests of unfairness vanish like confetti in a violent wind, for the fair and the unfair belong to the land of the moral; this is an existential island, ungoverned by the precepts of the mainland, autonomous from its comfort. It is no less unfair that we are ever favored in the first place; to lose the favor makes not a jot on the pages of ought.

We rightly call those dispossessed of a precious love or friendship, wretched. Perhaps the dissolution of friendship is even worse than that of love, being nobler in its essence. To lose it vexes both mind and heart, leaving us without recourse, ashamed of our loss because we are the ground of it. Yet, there are no lists in catechisms, no maxims of the wise, no precepts of religion, nor edicts of morality, which, if adhered to, would keep us from these agonies. The analysis is not intended to prescribe but to reveal. The loss of a friendship is not as base or as eclipsing as Gertrude's self-deceptive wretchedness. We seek to comprehend what it means to be wretched not to discover how to avoid it, since in some forms it may not be avoidable, but simply to contrast it with the fine so as to refine what the fine means.

This refinement is not the result of mere negation of what is wretched, as if by denying the one it is sufficient to affirm the other. What seems fundamental in wretchedness is that our own essential meaning is scorned by our own self-contempt; that the exile from where we belong is self-induced; that we ourselves point the finger of shame at the prisoner we have become. The fine affirm their own meaning, even and especially when they take responsibility; they welcome their own belonging rather than merely accept it casually; and in this belonging, they celebrate home by advocacy. Like the wretched, the fine cannot be spotted merely by moral precepts nor by sympathetic sentiments; they both confound the limitations of these legitimate endeavors, one dismally, the other radiantly.

The etymological origin of wretched as homeless suggests that its opposite, the fine, not only belongs but gathers the belonging together. Gertrude unfamilies her kin and unqueens her realm; a fine queen unifies the land; a fine mother assembles her brood into family. The fine are fine because they are not revered distantly as some transcending other but honored and embraced as our own. In this curious way, the fine become exemplar, perhaps even heroic.

The fine, as we have seen, are not the elite; as a consequence they do not disdain the individual commoner though they reject commonness, rather they transform the common into a shared welcome of belonging. To be fine is therefore never an entirely private matter. The fine are always themselves sources of refinement, as fine teachers not only instruct but embody learning. Conscious of themselves as radiating welcome, the fine heroically accept the burden and need of mastery, even though they are aware of their own finitude and imperfection. It is often overlooked that the heroic, in the strict sense, are not the mere beneficiaries of adulation for admirable deeds done in the past, but continually face the dreaded burden of being beyond their capacity; they suffer the fierce blindness of limelight and reverence, and, hence, are caught in a fateful burden that, as fateful, deserves neither praise nor censure, yet for which, as rooted in their own character, they must accept responsibility. It is in this sense that the wretched parallels even as it opposes the fine. Like those who are wretched, those who are fine are suspended between the culpable and inculpable, the praiseworthy and the merely envied, and for exactly the same kind of reason: the range of their existence expands beyond the culpability of actions, but this does not relieve the onus of responsibility. To refine oneself is to become fine and to become an exemplar, but as exemplar we find unachievable demands that we cannot help embrace but would gladly shun precisely because they are beyond our reach. Fine parents realize they may become objects of hero worship to their children, yet in anguish they dare not tell these precious learners all their own private faults lest they scandalize; fine teachers become mentors of the superior students but cannot disburden themselves of the roles that must be played; heroes must be all the more heroic in their flawed humanity as they inspire their admirers, for the cracks in the idol do not disbar idolatry. Just as the wretched queen is both origin and victim of her misery, so the fine are acutely aware that they themselves radiate what is greater than themselves. If the wretched can find solace neither in their misery nor their guilt, the fine can find no escape from their esteem nor their lack of desert for it. Yet the wretched inspire revulsion precisely because they are "guilty victims"—a seeming self-contradictory phrase—and the fine inspire adulation in their very reluctance to be esteemed beyond merit. The difference is that the wretched are alien to their own belonging, and the fine become welcomers beyond their welcome.

A juror is asked to do the impossible: to render a just verdict in the absence of the knowledge requisite to do so, which is why there is something both fine and wretched in a dutiful jury—fine because jury members perform in spite of their lack, since they must, and wretched for they alone bear the burden of an unfair responsibility. Here the wretchedness is merely felt, not assigned; it is countered by the nobility of their performing what in fact they have no capacity to do, yet in doing it they do not violate their worth but are welcomed by their heroism. As chapter 10 shows, this is possible only because of judgment.

To contrast the fine with the wretched seems to make the former enviable and the latter disagreeable, and thereby to suggest that perhaps the difference is merely one of eudaemonistic preference: it is simply more enjoyable being fine than wretched. It is possible to admit the eudaemonistic element, however, without making it the essential explanation. But why, even if this reason is not the motivational force or the essential meaning, is the fine personally more satisfying than the wretched? It cannot be pleasure or happiness, since the noble sufferer can be finer than the happily deceived. The present reflection shows that the role of exemplar inherent in being fine may well be unwanted and even burdensome. Granted no one would ever want to be wretched, but this rejection of wretchedness is not in itself sufficient to account for what attracts in being fine.

It is perhaps tempting to account for this by an appeal to the ideal: we find esteem in the struggle to achieve the unachievable when what is being sought is absolute and great; but this includes too much. There are probably a million young writers aspiring to achieve greatness in literary renown, but membership in this vast society in no way ensures that their idealizing makes them fine; indeed, we can halve the digits of that million and still find a populace far too wide to ascribe finery to them all. To participate in the struggle to achieve greatness may be a necessary but certainly is not a sufficient condition for the fine. It is not ideality, nor happiness, nor pleasure but joy that accounts for this preference. Joy is triumphant, in part because it is prepared by struggle, perhaps even defeat endured and hence defeated, but it is also an absorption of magnificence beyond ourselves, for in joy we are welcomed into the very sheltering that we revere as greater than ourselves. Joy, like wretchedness, is thus both earned and bestowed; its triumph over the base or the wretched relies on our struggle, but its embracing welcome is of a generosity that exceeds our deserving. This is paradoxical; but its very paradox is part of the joyousness of joy. Were it not paradoxical, joy would be merely elation. Neither pleasure, nor happiness, nor even idealistic struggle share this paradox;

but joy is the positive aspect whereas the feeling of wretchedness is the negative aspect of this paradox, and so joy alone is the existential preference for the fine.

This is not to say the fine are always joyous; it is merely to say that in the phenomenon of joy we discover how the fine radiates out from itself to assemble and bring together in welcome with leadership and authority. Thus, the wretched, in its self-loathing, scatters; the fine, in the joy of welcome, unifies. Self-loathing and its constituent element of self-hatred is of three levels: I can hate my private self, the institution of my belongings, and finally my species. To loath my own private existence is to torment myself with the ugly preference for my own rejection; to loath not myself but ourselves, when our own culture or nation is defiled as deserving contempt, is a form of existential betrayal or treason; to loath the very species as such, to reject the human race as mere pollutant of a planet, offensive to the animal kingdom because of its mastery, is a species of universal nihilism. There is no more miserable state than self-hatred, and these three levels can easily beguile us by the confusion of self-criticism, which is healthy, to self-loathing, which is diseased.

Contrasting these three levels of self-loathing are the three levels of joyous self-worth, which reveal what it means to be fine: the fine as singular person, the fine as communal, and the fine as vicar to the species—though these are not distinct phenomena, since to be a fine person gathers in welcome the fine community that as fine, mirrors the universal.

The opposition of the wretched to the fine, therefore, opens up a rich and wonderful paradox that now requires deep reflection. The ancient and esteemed problem of the relation between the specific individual and the universal, a problem that often seems as dry as the Gobi, as tasteless as tofu, and as dreary as the drone of pedantry, now becomes the focus of a most intense, existential confrontation.

Chapter 10

Judgment

> This royal throne of kings, this scept'red isle,
> This earth of majesty, this seat of Mars,
> This other Eden, demi-paradise,
> This fortress built by Nature for herself
> Against infection and the hand of war,
> This happy breed of men, this little world . . .
> This blessed plot, this earth, this realm, this England.
>
> —*Richard II*

> If I speak with the tongues of men and of angels and have not love I am as sounding brass and tinkling cymbal.
>
> —*1 Corinthians 13*

> We here highly resolve that these dead shall not have died in vain—that this nation under God, shall have a new birth of freedom—and that government of the people, by the people, for the people, shall not perish from the earth.
>
> —*Gettysburg Address*

Though familiar and perhaps in some senses true, these citations are troubling. Rather, it is precisely because they are true that they trouble. Only the scurrilous or pedantic would dismiss these three great segments of our heritage as mere emotional fluff. They speak universal truth and are admired by the sensitive and sensible throughout the world and throughout history. Yet their universal acclaim, though entirely justified, seems curiously at odds with their content. We are not all English, nor Christian, nor American; yet the English poet and the Christian saint and the American president, in their passionate eloquence of their own belonging, somehow accomplish a universal authority unreached and unreachable by mere abstractionist generality. We cannot substitute these specific references to England or Christianity or America with other communities. It is ludicrous to replace "England" with "Spain" in John of Gaunt's speech, or "love" with "obedience" in Paul's epistle, or "government of the people" with "revolutionary government by the party" in Lincoln's address. These are concrete, specific, irreplaceable institutions that bind with affection and passion; yet they undoubtedly speak universal truth—And that is the problem.

It is an ancient problem. At one time it was identified as the problem of the one and the many; at another, the problem of the particular and the universal; and since Kant, it has often been labeled the problem of judgment. Kant identifies the faculty or power by which we bring a particular under the lawlikeness of the universal as the faculty of judgment. Whatever its name, there is a time-honored problem in relating what is specific to the rules that govern it. To raise the problem in terms of how these three quotations seem to affect all of us even if we do not partake in the specific institutions of the speaker may, however, seem a highly unusual and even quixotic approach. Perhaps it is even backward, since it may seem the answer to this formulation must first depend on how we understand the more general question of particulars and universals. Yet, it is precisely because we, as a general audience, nevertheless do find meaning in these very particularist assertions that the problem may find in this novel formulation a more concrete, and surely fresher, analysis. We do dwell in the world as both concrete and universal, and that we somehow manage to find in specific instances a universality that gives authority to its meaning deserves reflection. That the present formulation is raised in terms of how seemingly local advocacy achieves reckoning on the most ample reaches of our understanding, opens the possibility that perhaps our inquiry into the fine may itself be furthered even as it throws light on one among the most venerable of the vexing questions.

The temptation to seek redress from this vexation by the dismissive appeal to mere emotion can and should be resisted. We need not deny that it is the eloquence or even passion of these citations that helps to render them memorable and quotable; it is merely enough to recognize that eloquence need not invalidate the truth of a passage; and that it is even possible the very eloquence of the passage itself constitutes a part of its truth. The threefold unity of self as individual, member, and species, denied in the self-hatred that is wretched and affirmed in the welcoming that is fine, now offers itself as a philosophically promising methodology. Somehow, in the refining that gathers, the sharp distinctions between I and we and we and all can be thought together. If it is the refinement of being who I am that welcomes who we are, and who we are, as refined, mirrors all the entire species, the advancing, widening dialectic of the fine itself must now be tested. But first, the full range and power of the question must be assayed.

Only as a jubilant, passionate Christian could Paul have refined the small gatherings of this new advocacy into a universal church. Not normally eloquent—indeed as a writer he suffered from fairly ungentle prose and crude syntax—he managed in his epistle to the Corinthians to refine his own zeal to a binding or welcoming that established, and not merely described, a unity among his fellow advocates. It is the truth of his welcome that gives it its eloquence, and not merely the eloquence that persuades us to believe it as true. Thus, it is the refinement of the message that establishes its truth. Does this mean that because of Paul's eloquence Christianity is the only true religion? It seems outrageous to say so. Yet, there is truth, and not mere personal belief, in the realization that love is a ranking virtue, and Paul as Christian shows us this by the simple technique of contrasting the distinctively Christian virtue of love over and against the very eloquence of speaking with the tongues of angels and of men. Non-Christians obviously hear this and affirm it as true; but in affirming it they enter into the gathering that makes them welcome as Christian. This seems to suggest it is the specificity of the message as Christian and not its trans-Christian, universal availability that matters. Why, then, does the universality matter at all?

The thought, the fervor, and the language itself are fine, and as such can and often do refine the hearer. Perhaps, then, it is the refinement that universalizes the concrete; perhaps the fine translates the local dialect into the authority of dialectic. If this is so, it is our own threefoldreality—I, we, and all—that must be tortured to reveal the secret that refines.

Lincoln's speech reflects Lincoln's problem, and Lincoln's problem echoes the problem of this chapter. He believed in the Union, not in the North; yet it was the North's will and power, then strained by factions, dubiety, weariness, and confusion, that needed the refining unity to sustain the defining conflict. What a paradox was there. Denied the one, natural appeal available to most wartime leaders, that we on our side are worthier than they on theirs, Lincoln had to stir the North to the nobility of sacrifice in order to keep open the welcome to the rebellious peoples of the South. He had to separate on the most fundamental level of conquerer and defeated in order to rejoin them as one. That he succeeded is found not only in the pages of history but in a two-minute masterpiece of oratory. For the term *we* here has a double referent: those in the North sacrificing and struggling, and the Union itself, both North and South. It is the reunited Union of free people and a people's government that sustain the costly effort. The very delicacy of the challenge facing Lincoln particularizes his speech to the point of uniqueness; the complexity of it is so singular that it seems to have no peer and no possibility of generality. Since there is no other occasion even vaguely like Lincoln's staggering challenge, how can it serve to illuminate us all? We cannot humiliate the power of the address by marking it merely as an instance of the concept of patriotism that, as abstract and nonspecific, is available to all. For again, it is the very specificity of it that makes it so fine. An abstract appeal to universal principles would not have sustained the nation, and Lincoln's use of distinct identifiers makes this clear: it is *we* who have come *here* to *this* battlefield to honor *these* dead. That these dead include both Union and Confederate troops simply makes the problem more staggering.

The address, to an assembled few, unified a whole country by strengthening only a part of it, and in so doing spoke to the entire world. This cannot be accounted for by the mere subsumption of this unique speech under broad, abstract principles, for it is the uniqueness of the speech, entirely lacking in abstract universals, that gives it its power and authority. How are we to understand this?

Perhaps one way to come to grips with the problem is by focusing on the first of the three passages; for unlike Paul's appeal as Christian and Lincoln's as American, we find that Shakespeare appeals as artist, and as such is already in the realm of universality. Art, it is claimed, transcends local boundaries and provincial interests just because, as art, it does not proselytize but simply pleases. If *Richard II* can be seen as a universal artwork, perhaps the passages by Paul and Lincoln can be seen in a similar manner: their eloquence makes them art, and as such, they are judged because of how they please us and delight our emotions, not because they persuade us to action or to devotion to a particular cause. Art itself, through refinement, allows us to see in the particular what is universally meaningful, and it is for this reason that Kant considers our aesthetic and artistic responses only as reflective judgments. The mere artistry of *Richard II* does not forfeit its particularity: Gaunt's speech is still about England—it could not be made about France or Brazil. The fact that Brazilians and Frenchmen can still appreciate the play is precisely what the problem is about. We do not pretend that Lincoln's speech was a prod to resolve the spirit of Americans in 1864, but thereafter was considered a mere artwork enjoyed solely because of its fine language. Even if all three passages be allocated to useless museums, that is, bracketed by the protective guardians of picture frames or quotation marks that remove art from the practical world, we are still left with the troubling issue of the peculiar nature of judgment itself: how do we universalize the particular? How do we find in local advocacy, such as Paul's Christianity, Lincoln's America, and Shakespeare's England, any authority beyond that of the particular or specific institution?

The term *authority* itself is suggestive, for we distinguish authority from brute coercion or simple terror. In a civilized society, laws have authority beyond their mere enforcement by the police, especially if they are passed by governmental institutions that support their enactment with publicly aired reasons based on moral principles. Perhaps, then, the way or ways in which laws have authority rather than power can help illuminate the general problem of particularity and universality.

Laws, we recognize, are by definition universal. The law prohibiting murder applies to each and every citizen. Yet, exactly what constitutes murder cannot ever be adequately denoted, however precise the language, by statute alone. The statute is interpreted first in its execution and then in its judiciary implementation, which gives rise to the three branches of government: legislative, executive, judiciary. For some, the interpretive power of the judiciary seems to make it supreme: the law is as the court decides. Further, the court seems to be the one branch of government that directly concerns the citizens, protecting them from the possible despotism of the executive and the arbitrariness of the legislature. The fact that in many cases judges and justices are appointed for life emphasizes their elevation above the fray of political wrangling and undue influence; no other officers of the state have lifetime appointments sequestered from the dreary demands of representation and election.

Is there not a danger here that judges, as both interpreters of the law and as the most concrete and final contact with the individual citizen, may become tyrants of the bench? If laws must be interpreted as well as measured by the courts, are not judges, as final arbiters, the only true executors and legislators? There are moments when the judiciary indeed usurps authority, especially when the other branches become weak, and as a consequence there has been true judicial tyranny. For the most part we do not see the judiciary as dangerously autonomous; though the law must be interpreted and applied in order for law to be more than mere statute, the legislative authority to enact statutes is not thereby weakened. It may be difficult to see where the interpretation of the law differs from the making of the law, but the distinction is necessary for the law to have authority. Merely because I judge does not mean my judging is the same as my legislating. Indeed, to judge at all requires the lawlike authority of legislation; I cannot judge without universality, but the judging itself is always particular.

Certain laws themselves are justified solely on the basis of judgmental authority as opposed to mere determination of behavior. Every modern state has laws prohibiting sexual intimacy with minors, sometimes referred to as statutory rape. The reasoning behind such laws is impressive. If the age of consent is eighteen, as it is in many American states, the argument is that the young girl (or boy), because of her age, is simply unable to consent. Rape may be defined as a carnal act without consent; but if a sixteen year old claims to consent, the state refuses to accept her apparent willingness because, although she may have knowledge, and she may well desire to be intimate, she is incapable of the judgment necessary for true consent. The girl may indeed be quite intelligent; she may have taken courses in biology and psychology so that she knows even more than the seducing adult what happens physically; she may even have learned from reading about the psychology of sex that the emotions often cloud judgment; she may even know that her own desire to be popular is a compelling reason for her submission. Thus, she is not lacking in knowledge. The state still wisely argues that truly informed consent (i.e., judgment) is not possible for one so young. A certain amount of experience with one's own emotions and emotional history must be presupposed in order for the understanding to be deep enough to warrant true consent. This law, in other words, recognizes as a fact, and incorporates this fact into the very justification of the law, that to qualify as a consenting adult, judgment must be assumed.

There is not only judgment within this law, but judgment in the making of it. No one is so naive as to believe that on midnight of the eve of her eighteenth birthday the girl suddenly is transformed into a mature woman capable of consent. The statutory precision of the birthdate is surely arbitrary, even as it is necessary for its enforcement. But it is not entirely arbitrary, for in the judgment of the legislators, possibly echoing the common judgment of the populace, this age requirement seems generally apt; our experience and reflection, and our own memory of our own youthful vulnerability, deem the statutory age-limit to be as encased in the law. The reasoning behind the law, therefore, recognizes the inevitability of judgment. This is truly remarkable, for the legal argumentation is based on the notion that the minor can decide, in some sense, but not yet judge; but the adult is sufficient unto herself to judge and no longer needs the protection of law. The adult woman is capable of judgment, and simply because of this the law cannot intrude. The difference between the minor and the adult is not knowledge, but judgment, and the condition for being able to judge is a certain amount of lived experience, measured by time. The young girl must, in other words, be able to refine herself by reflection and experience in order to become who she is. In learning, she becomes who she is, and with this refined understanding, she no longer needs the protection of law against her own vulnerability. The judgment by the lawmakers is about the judgment of the girl. The law, therefore, is law because judgment is possible.

The same can be said for interpreting a text. Texts cannot be unjudged, a point the deconstructionists have in their favor; but neither can the reading or interpretation be sovereign over what is written, a fact that defangs most of what is radical in deconstruction, and, hence, unfortunately, most of what is provocative and even interesting about it. Pianists interpret Mozart and actors interpret Shakespeare, yet we judge a pianist harshly who fails to show us Mozart and an actor unworthy who violates the integrity of Shakespeare. So-called literal interpreters of scripture rarely are so—a medieval sect interpreted Christ's maxim to be as little children so radically that grown men went about in diapers and played with rattles. We know, however, this is not what is meant by the passage, and we judge these now defunct sectarians as foolish. At the same time, scriptural interpreters who recast the texts of their faith merely to accommodate their own changing ideology raise doubt as to why they need the text at all.

In all these cases, from the jurist to musician, from actor to textual interpreter, the stark phenomenon seems inescapable: laws and principles are formally vacuous without applicatory and interpretive judgment, yet this realization does not undermine the authority of the stated norms, nor does it license judges to be entirely free of them. A moment's reflection also shows us we cannot resolve this paradox by the discovery of some superalgorithms that, by the application of a decision procedure tell us how to judge. (Here are the ten commandments, and here are ten megacommandments telling us how to apply and interpret the original ten.)

If judging, as Kant suggests, links the universality of the maxim or statute to the uniqueness of the individual in the world, and if this alone is lawlikeness or living under law, and if not all judges (or actors or players or interpreters) are equal, then it seems we must be able to judge judges. Is this a violation of good sense? Are we engaged in a slippery slope? The point makes itself: of course we judge judges. A judge, who interprets the laws of Congress, can himself be impeached by Congress; we can judge interpreters of Mozart or Shakespeare as bad interpreters, and we can do these things without assuming hidden principles or metaalgorithms precisely because as judgments they are not themselves algorithmic nor are they principles or rules. This does not deny the truth or validity of some absolute rules, nor does it deny that in making a judgment we must be guided by principles that are universal and constant; it merely distinguishes judgment from decision procedures.

How then do we judge judges? We think about them as learned, wise, experienced, insightful, and penetrating—somehow embodying who we are as exemplars. There is admittedly a species of benign circularity here: we learn truth from the wise, yet we acknowledge them as wise only because they do reveal truth. This is possible because of the priority of learning (as refinement of who we are) over knowledge. If we already knew clearly in advance what eloquence reveals, we would not be learning but merely recognizing what we already know; but if the eloquence confronts our imprecision with the painful, piercing insight of what we are able to discover as true, we embrace it as our own precisely because it welcomes in its revelatory discovery. We honor Paul not because he is the guaranteed keeper of hidden truths that we must accept simply because whatever he says is true, but because, in the fervor of his local advocacy, he uncovers what is true and makes it universally acceptable. The personal or local advocacy is an essential part of this judgmental learning; it is not a mere access to truth but an integral part of truth itself, for judging is neither the private instincts of an individual nor the lawlike abstraction of principle, but rather that which, as broader than either, gathers them together as welcoming. This welcoming, however, is the result of a refinement along the following dialectical lines:

As I become refined, I become no longer a mere private individual but a vicar to my own belonging. In this process of learning, to be who I am expands into being who we are. When we are further refined, we become mirrors to all. Thus, the dialectic of learning proceeds through the refinement from privacy to vicarage and from vicarage to mirroring. This is not the language of the resulting judgments, which as distinct from the judges become mere propositions or maxims, but only of judging in the sense of being a judge. To say we become vicars of what is our own, and then, as vicars, to become mirrors of the species, is to speak entirely in the modes of what it means to be who we are as being able to become refined. This dialectic is not inevitable; not all who are Americans are refined in their being American to be a vicar of America, and even fewer are able in their vicarage to mirror the species. Only the fine American is vicar to the nation, and only the finest vicars are mirrors of the species. To shrink from the possibility of belonging is to become wretched, to refine the belonging as specific vicars and specific cultural mirrors is to learn and, hence, to become fine.

The fine, as learned rather than as knowing, refined rather than crass or vulgar, itself is not accounted for solely by the subsumption under principle. We must assume principle else we could not even engage in the quest for the fine; but what matters here is the modality of being principled rather than being guided solely by private interests. The articulated maxims or propositions that are stated principles do indeed matter, but they are dependent on the more fundamental modality of being principled. In chapter 9, we discovered it is possible to hate ourselves in three ways, as I, as we, and as all; it is also possible to rejoice as I, we, and all. These are not three distinct entities, nor is their hierarchy determined merely by the arithmetic but solely and entirely by refinement. What we call judgment is, then, not the subsumption of the specific ur der the governance of the universal, but the refinement of self as individual to self as member and ultimately to self as species. The dialectic or movement from individual to member is vicarage, and from member to species is mirroring. Thus Paul, as zealous and sacrificial, inspired by the truth of the message, is vicar; and ennobled by that truth to fine eloquence, he lets that vicarage mirror the universality of the species.

It is the middle step that seems to confound most formalist thinkers. Why, they ask, is Paul's Christianity even significant? Surely Paul the man could have realized the significance of love and simply stated it as a universally valid proposition. There seems no necessity to include his being Christian as a part of that truth. It is precisely because Lincoln's speech stirs all sensitive readers throughout the world that his being American, which millions who read the speech are not, need play no role in our understanding of its truth. It seems formally sufficient to have the universal truth spoken by the individual without the need of some mediating institution. Why not go directly from individual *I* to universal *all*?

To deny the middle step—to dispense with judgment altogether and merely direct the individual by means of the formality of the law—is to reify two abstractions: the individual and the law. To be an individual is merely to exist in an already shared belonging— our home—in terms of one's privacy and particularity as entities within the broadest expansion of abstraction—the world. There is no individual who is not already a son or daughter, brother or sister, citizen, member, sectarian, and dweller. For an individual even to come to grips with the meaning of universality and lawlikeness requires an already inherited language, rich with cultural persuasions, a tradition of critique, and a sense of uniqueness and personal significance that only the most fertile and welcoming of traditions can provide. Indeed, any meaningful sense of individual rests upon the prior notion of respect, without which an individual is nothing more than a numerical unit. But respect, as is discovered early in this quest, is what characterizes the fine from the vulgar, either as crass or as elite. Self-respect, denied in the wrangle of the wretched, depends on the esteem of one's belonging and not on hermit's isolation from welcoming. It is thus the middle or judg- that gathers the universal with the individual. This mid- Lincoln's Americanism, Paul's Christianity, and land, is therefore prior to, and the ultimate, explanation of both world as universal and particular as individual. *In medio stat* not only *virtus* but also *realitas*.

The fine cannot be determined by rules, maxims, or decision procedures; it can only be judged. Yet judgment itself is a species of refinement. The unrefined as wretched is entirely without judgment; and lacking judgment is thereby crass, vulgar, and common. We do not determine that Emily Dickinson is a fine poet by the assignment of preexisting criteria; rather, we judge her as a fine poet and in so doing appeal to the universality of her truth. But her poetry itself is also a source of our own refinement, without which we could not judge her as fine. So the fine is judged as fine, but to be able to judge is itself made possible by refinement. Accordingly, the dialectic of refinement provides a response—perhaps the finest response—to an ancient question: how do we make sense of the one and the many, the universal and the particular? But judging itself—that by which we realize the internal connection of the particular and the universal—is needed to discern the fine. I must be refined in order to judge and can only recognize or achieve the fine by means of judgment. To ask which comes first is to think in terms of first and second in time, or to appeal to necessary and sufficient conditions, both of which are nonjudgmental functions and, hence, do not apply. This is what it means to say that learning is a refinement of who we are. The wretched, as opposed to the fine, cannot judge and thus cannot learn.

Chapter 11

The Philosopher as Fine

With the realization that refinement lies at the base of judgment, the climber's trek seems to have reached a mountaintop. This assault upon the heights began with the remarkable discovery that perception itself can be refined, and peaks with the achievement that the true antithesis to the fine is wretchedness. The wretched are incapable of judgment; and judgment itself is a species of refinement. In this development, the basic metaphor was that of the mountain climber, reaching with ever-increasing labor the elusive but alluring heights. There may remain even higher peaks that surround this crest, to be sure, but they beckon beyond the inquiry.

The original metaphor was not of a climb, however, but of a knightly quest. The mountain was scaled perforce since it lay in the path; and to some extent the achievement of its height is worthy of the effort. But romantic tales of medieval knights in search of some holy grail—truth, in this case—are rarely triumphant. The wisdom of these tales seems to lie in the realization that it is the trek itself that transforms the knight; that the grail, perhaps briefly glimpsed in some mystic cave or wood, is never brought home to the point of departure and possession. It is the learning and not the knowing that matters. A point temporarily occluded in the mists and snows of the climb, now reemerges on the higher elevation. We recall learning of Antony's preciousness only when Cleopatra has forever lost him. It is the dreadful failure that reveals; sad wisdom seems the deepest; we are enlightened only by our shadows and unsuccess succeeds.

This is not a pessimism or even a frustration with our limits. The quest for the grail does indeed transform the knight even as it thwarts his possession of the sacred object; and this transformation, from vulgarity to refinement, may well matter more than the success in sequestering the grail in a captive box. Yet, it is still a hard truth—which is why toughness is cited as a mark of the fine. Refinement makes the seeker not more delicate but tougher; yet it is a toughness that renders us more sensitive to the subtler pains of learning. Only the tough endure enough to learn from suffering rather than merely to howl, as do the wretched, in lamentation. The returning knight, grailless, has conquered more than he set out to win, though not all knights are made tough enough by their trek to learn this wisdom.

This may seem but a trite recall of the adages of our youth, a bland retasting of theopablum that needs no teeth to make it palatable. Where is the refined seasoning, the enhanced flavor, in these banal tidbits of folk wisdom? Is it possible that the tiny seeds of royal flavor were simply swallowed whole by the child, and only with the molars of maturity can these seeds be ground to release their savor? Is not all inquiry a refinement in this sense? A child knows that five and three equals eight; the philosopher retastes the truth of this and achieves wonder: it is not merely true that five and three are eight, it is now astounding, for we seek to comprehend how it is possible we can do such a thing. So the adventures of the questing knight may contain a seemingly banal message, but for the refinement that is philosophy, truth is never trite. Indeed, as we see in the analysis of the elitist, sophisticated disdain for the common is merely a species of vulgarity. That the elusiveness of the grail, or the tardiness of our realization of Antony's preciousness, is painful, does not demote the nobility of the quest, for the trek can toughen and hence refine the learner.

What does it mean, then, that the fine is often learned or achieved only through the failure of the original search? Does this mean the original urgency is deceptive, that knights are simply naive or stupid in believing there is a grail at all, and their enlightenment is merely the uncovering of their superstition? If the knight were truly knightly, ought he not to have realized the quest was not for some illusory grail but the discovery of his own inner strength? Even if we admit the need for such illusion as a necessarily heuristic propaedeutic, are we not still compelled, at the end of the quest, to realize the grail all along was but a fiction? Must we not, at the end of the play, simply indict Cleopatra for the giddiness of her earlier adolescent rapture, and limply wish she had been more mature at the beginning so as to have avoided the tragedy at the end?

It is not superstition for the child to realize that five and three equal eight. Philosophical astonishment does not gainsay this; it simply reveals the truth as more remarkable. For the grail to reveal its truth by its elusive mystery does not render the grail a fiction. It is neither stupid nor adolescent for Cleopatra to be addled by the dizziness of eros; it is magnificent.

It is nevertheless encumbant on this inquiry to probe deeply into the final mysteries inherent in the quest for the fine. We need not deny the reality of the grail in order to learn from the failed quest a refinement of who we are. Indeed, as the reflections on judgment show, it is only because the grail (or truth) is real that the failure to corral it can refine the searcher. The penetrating analyses of the fine have uncovered already unexpectedly rich contributions to many of the established domains of the philosopher, suggesting perhaps that the study of the fine and its opposites may provide a hitherto untapped methodology for thinking about the great problems that rightly trouble us. But now the method itself is tested as it tests what may be the most troubling of all questions that we can possibly ask: why are we troubled at all? What does it mean to question and to be troubled? We quest; but why need we? If the trek for any grail, especially truth, is arduous, does this not suggest something already is awry? Perhaps, like Richard, we are all

> Cheated, of feature by dissembling nature,
> Deform'd, unfinish'd, sent before my time
> Into this breathing world scarce half made up, . . .
>
> (I, 1)

In other words, is not the most fundamental question ever, of all time, this: why we are finite and flawed, but only through refinement toward the flawless can we illuminate who we are? If we are, albeit to a lesser extent than Richard, sent by a deceitful nature only half made up, and hence can only crawl piteously toward truth and ever be denied its full possession, then *why* we are doomed to trek haunts all other trekking. *Search* for the truth? What truth is shown in this? That we are only searchers? Why is this nature (or this God?) so dissembling, so cheating? Is it possible that the quest for the fine may enable us to throw light upon the latent question that haunts every question: why must I question at all?

We know we are not all-wise; that is the brute and given reality. Neither are we entirely bereft of knowledge. It seems we have just enough knowledge to realize we are cheated; perhaps then we should lament our knowledge. Squid and porcupine seem too stupid to realize they are stupid and, hence, are content. Why did not God make us smarter? Or, if contentment ranks, why has he not made us dumber? However smarter we may be, we could always wonder why we were not even smarter, unless of course we were infinitely so, all-knowing, godlike. Should we complain we are not God? And not being God, should we disdain our existence absolutely and become nihilists, or cooly, rationally, indifferent? Perhaps there is nothing worthwhile in being less than infinite. Wherein lies the worth in being discontentedly less than all-wise?

We can ask this question seriously, as a question, without taking on the quality of ingratitude or spoiled truculence. What is wisdom anyway? In philosophical history we discover that wisdom is not the same as knowledge; indeed, it is not even a kind of superknowledge of certain great mysteries; it is rather, according to the Greeks, a virtue. In modern argot (that confuses taxonomy with truth), we say wisdom is not an epistemological but an ethical term. To be wise is to be virtuous—that is, it is to live in such a way as to make a finite life worth living. Very well, then—what does the virtue, wisdom, mean? Plato suggests, in the *Republic*, it is that virtue in which truth is revered for its own sake and not merely for its practical, applicatory value. Like beauty, which need not service beyond itself to be of worth, truth need not be ranked solely by its usefulness.

But if wisdom consists in revering truth for its own sake, then the greater question now emerges in all its stupefying magnitude: why ever should we consider this a virtue? In what way does the adoption of this reverence for truth make a less-than-perfect existence worthwhile? Why not rather be, like the squid, unwise and content?

If truth be intrinsically worthwhile, it cannot consist of answers, either discovered or as yet undiscovered. For if truth is merely the collection of the correct answers to all possible and meaningful questions, its worth is nothing other than our ignorance, for once a question is answered, it is no longer a question. Truth is not the possession of knowledge, since knowledge just is the state in which the question no longer provokes. To love answers is thus not the same as to love truth. But this itself seems puzzling: are not all questions merely manifestations of ignorance about possible terminating answers? If I question (or ask) whether the milk is sour, and testing it find it to be so, there is no question any more. Answering eradicates the question; it cannot even *be* in any sense.

Not all questioning is of this sort. It is possible to question in such a way as to retain the wonder of what is sought as well as the wonder of the seeking itself, as lovers ache to learn more of their beloved without wishing their mystery to disappear. The point is not that some answers permit terminal resolution and others permit further answering, but that the questioning itself is fundamentally different. The love of truth for its own sake is a virtue precisely because such esteem alone allows for the questioning that seeks solace in a learning that will never ebb. Any extrinsic evaluation of truth must by its very nature permit a terminus however distant. It is precisely this denial that our questing matters only if we in fact identify and lay hold of a terminal answer, that makes wisdom a virtue. For by questing in this way, we realize that our existence, as both self-reflective yet finite, does not depend on the notion of service or purpose to justify it. Wisdom breaks the hegemony of the first kind of questioning in which terminating answers end the quest and makes room for the second kind of questioning, which is self-justifying. It is better (i.e., finer) to quest after truth for its own sake because in such questing the seeker need not reach beyond truth to some externalist success, inevitably denied him, to warrant his seeking. Neither does such questing become a mere self-serving endeavor, as children playing on a carousel never get anywhere but simply enjoy going around in a circle. The quest for truth is not a quest for questing, else we could not say truth matters.

There is a natural propensity to seek explanations of things by locating them in their proper context of a broader reality, as we explain the mainspring in the watch by its role in making the watch run, and then explain the watch in terms of its usefulness in telling time, and the telling of time in terms of making life more efficient, and an efficient life itself as serving the society, and so on. Rarely are explanations other than this. We even ask, feigning profundity, what our purpose in life is, as if having a purpose—that is, being in the service of something other than ourselves—is somehow more intelligible than not. To revere truth as having no purpose beyond itself breaks the dictatorship of this kind of explanation. Its intrinsic worth makes truth supremely significant; in this realization we no longer must account for everything by its function. We need not ask what our purpose is but can ask what our meaning is.

If wisdom, as the reverence for truth for its own sake, is a virtue, we must ask more deeply what virtue means; and since this question is raised in Greek terms, reflection on the Greek meaning may be required. We may gain insight by asking the opposite: what is a vice? As we have seen, anything that enslaves, particularly anything that is self-enslaving, is vicious. To be a slave to base desires is a vice, as love of money enslaves us in the vice of avarice, capitulation to fear enslaves by the vice of cowardice, weakness for self-eclipse enslaves by the vice of drunkenness, loss of dignity enslaves by the vice of wantonness. Perhaps the most fundamental vice, therefore, is that by which we understood ourselves as slaves: namely, that our very existence is necessarily thought of solely in terms of service or dependence on some grander reality. Only if we can learn to think nonmechanistically can this radical vice be overcome. But unless thinking is grounded in truth there can be no such overcoming, for if we ground thinking in anything other than truth we are deluded, and being deluded is also a vice since it enslaves us to the false. The independence of thinking from mere calculating achievement is possible only if truth by itself matters. Thus, the intrinsic worth of truth is the ground of all virtue.

To love truth for its own sake is the virtue of wisdom. But from whence comes this ability to love truth? It is the love of truth rather than mere truth isolated from our seeking it that seems to set us free. Do we then love the very love of truth? If wisdom loves truth, what loves wisdom itself? The term *philosophy* is precise: it is the love of wisdom; consequently it is the love of the loving of truth. How is this doubling of the affection thinkable? Is there the danger of a regress? It would seem the virtuous, in their direct love of truth, are superior to the philosopher who loves the virtue that consists in loving truth. To love the virtue of wisdom does not demote the actual love of truth itself; but the problem persists. Why is wisdom a virtue, that is, why does it make life worth living to revere truth for its own sake? And if loving truth is indeed a virtue, why does the love of that virtue for its own sake make the philosopher? There is no greater response to these questions—and we note the term *response* as opposed to *answer*—than what is provided for us by Plato's myth of the cave in the *Republic*. We must, however, rethink this myth with careful reverence for its dramatic and revealing qualities.

The story is familiar. A prisoner, fettered from birth within a cave in such a way as to see only shadows thrown on a wall by a fire, is released; he, then, with his new painfully won freedom, discovers that his earlier state was deceptive; that what he had thought were real things were actually only shadows, caused by cutout figures of ordinary objects being moved in front of the fire. The prisoner is then moved outside the cave entirely where he may observe real things in the real world, illumined not by false fires but by the sun; after this he is forced to reenter the cave.

Such a simple, direct, and revealing image has an unusually powerful effect; at the same time it has produced such wildly variant interpretations that it is sometimes hard to believe the scholars read the same text. Perhaps the very wealth of the imagery invites multiple readings. Perhaps, too, the image strikes so deep a chord in readers because it reveals truth so profoundly. In any event, it deserves a respect that cannot gainsay critique; if we are to learn about learning we must recognize the essential quality of dramatic conflict inherent in the search for wisdom. This realization pinpoints two important characteristics of the cave myth that are often overlooked or even denied. The first is that the myth is a metaphor for learning and not a mere taxonomy of kinds of knowledge; the second is the deep, philosophical significance of Plato's dramaturgy, often given only lip service by academic scholars who know far more about reading texts than confronting drama. We know the myth is about learning or education because Plato explicitly identifies his story in this way; it is also consistent within the development of the whole dialogue, especially from book 5 through book 8, in which the central question is raised about allowing the lover of learning (philomathes) to become a lover of wisdom (philosophes). The educational interpretation requires a careful rereading of the text along the lines consistent with the theme that learning is self-refinement. But it is the dramatic character that deserves our first reflection.

Many contemporary scholars are beginning to realize that the dramatic element in Plato's dialogues deserves further consideration than has traditionally been given it. Unfortunately, the predominant approach usually seems to mean by this adopting one of two rather simplistic views: the first is that Socrates already knows the answer to the question being asked in each dialogue but has a devilish time communicating it to a remarkably dense audience. The second sees

Socrates as the embodiment of the virtue being discussed, showing us the virtue in a way that no propositional account or essentialist definition can accommodate. That is, on the one hand, we are supposed to believe that Socrates knows perfectly well what courage is, but given the obdurance or even outright stupidity of Laches and Nicias, fails to get them to realize it. (Why Socrates, if he were to know the definition, does not simply tell us, is explained by vague appeals to "method" or the attempt to get the generals to think for themselves.) On the other hand, we are asked to believe Socrates himself is unable to isolate a sufficiently precise definition of courage, but actually manifests it in his character: he is courageous, not only in the actual battle that precedes the dialogue but also in the way he carries out the inquiry. Given these two possible readings, the role that drama plays is one of method. It either provides the irritating procedure of provoking the audience to think, or it shows us a sterling, near-saintly character that, by the so-called dramatic method, reveals the model of the virtues. Both of these readings are unsatisfactory, for neither is truly dramatic at all.

We must not forget who Plato's contemporaries are. This was the age of Pericles and the generation immediately following. The chief dramatists were Aeschylus, Sophocles, and Euripides—among the very greatest in the entire history of mankind; perhaps only Shakespeare equals them in the tragic genre. How does the character of Socrates match up dramatically to the likes of Agammemnon, Oedipus, and Medea? The one thing Attic audiences realized was that to make a good drama one must have a tormented, complex hero who is agonized by a very real, perhaps insoluable question. Antigone is forced by circumstances beyond her control to choose between two unacceptable alternatives: offend her kingly uncle or the gods. Either way she must fail. Her sister Ismene chooses to obey the king, and she is almost forgotten by play's end. It is not her choice, but the magnificence of her character in facing up to her choice that sears the hot brand of Antigone's name forever in our hearts and memories. Jocasta, like Ismene, prefers to retreat from the conflict; she begs her husband to stop inquiring into who he really is. The passion for truth tears Oedipus apart: we witness this noble denuding while truth is palpably being revealed counter to all our human preferences. Like Antigone, Oedipus is caught: untruth is unworthy, but learning truth is terrible. Orestes must, as a noble youth, avenge his father's murder; but this means killing his own mother. What does this do to him? What does it do to us, the audience? The characters within these mighty plays are neither embodiments of particular virtues nor saints, even by Greek standards; but they are noble because they greatly confront great torment. In order for this to occur as a drama, the genius of Aeschylus, Sophocles, and Euripides presented their characters not as one- or even two-dimensional models, but as multidimensional, both good and bad, strong and weak. They are heroic in the sense of revealing the wealth of our humanity by overreaching it in the agony of the conflict, not by solving it or knowing it or even by moral superiority in doing what one's conscience dictates. (Indeed, it is Cassandra, not a tragic figure but a pathetic one, who can see into the future, but as Hecuba points out, neither her suffering nor her knowledge makes her wise.)

With such outstanding models, what does it mean to interpret Socrates as a dramatic character? If he is the unruffled, saintlike embodiment of the virtues, then he is antidramatic, for where is the conflict within? If he knows but cannot tell, then he is just incompetent: modern dictionaries do a much better job of "defining" the virtues. If he knows, but deliberately refuses to tell, and merely drops hints as crumbs leading to a sugar-house, then he is a con artist or worse, a mystical gnostic. Incredibly, each of these insulting models have legions of scholarly defenders. It is perhaps not surprising that this should be so, since even the literary scholars trivialize by reading the great tragedies as psychological, ideological, or even moral messages. *Othello* is seen as a message warning us against jealousy, *Hamlet* is seen as a warning against contemplative hesitancy or loving our mothers too much. Luckily, in the case of the actual tragedies, the performances themselves when experienced sweep away these banal indecencies with a mighty passion, leaving us profoundly moved by their truth.

What, then, does it mean to suggest the dialogues are truly dramatic? Perhaps Socrates, in his critique of Athens, is deeply disturbed by his own seeming impiety, and his confrontation with Euthyphro is not to show that the young man is wrong or even impious, but that Socrates himself may be. Euthyphro would then be more like Jocasta or Ismene: less agonized by his dilemma, seeking refuge in nonquestioning. In the *Phaedo*, the fear of misology, addressed by Simias and Cebes, surely is a wrenching confrontation for one who reveres reason: perhaps it is unreasonable to be reasonable. The dialogues thereby become not dictionaries in disguise nor clever hagiographies, but philosophical dramas in which thinking itself is tortured by its own character and inevitability. Just as Antigone and Orestes become victims of their own fate, so Socrates is dramatically tormented by his own philosophical modality: not an embodiment of virtues but an embodiment of the tortured confrontation with the problematic of the virtues, particularly wisdom.

There is certainly such torment in the *Republic*. Is not the Athenian, Socrates, at odds with his own country when espousing the virtues of what seems to be a Spartan state? In urging the young lovers of learning to seek truth is he not threatening the very authority of the tradition that the state is supposed to provide? Is not philosophy by its nature inconsistent with governmental and religious authority? Is not the love of justice at odds with the love of truth? The myth of the cave is in fact a drama within a drama and needs to be read as such. The released prisoner in Plato's myth can be seen as dramatic—and, hence, as truly philosophical—only if care be taken in confronting the cruel refining of each step. It is needful to realize that the fettered prisoner's life prior to his release is indeed a pleasant one. He has companionship, he can deal successfully with the world, and he is at peace. We are told later that what he sees are but shadows. Yet, the food he sees and eats sustains him, the house he sees protects him from the elements, the roses he smells delight his senses, and the clothes he wears hides his nakedness and keeps him warm. Why then are they not real? Perhaps more important, what difference does it make if they are but shadows since they provide him with the necessities and pleasures of life? No wonder he is reluctant to be "set free" since this is a familiar and successful world.

It is the first step of release that truly matters. Once we discover that our previous images were cast by the light of a bonfire, the critical is triumphant. We realize the fire now represents certain fundamental presuppositions of how we look at the world. But this realization that there is something artificial about the unexamined life is painful precisely because we seem to lose the immediacy of piety; the brightness even of the artificial light hurts the eyes; we have lost the comfortable belonging with our friends and family; and already the capacity to distinguish the subtle distinctions among the shadows is waning.

The freedom from the original chains disadvantages us in practical, everyday discourse. A dangerous error is to read the first emancipation as a rejection of the cultural and religious teachings that are learned while still chained before the wall. The released prisoner does not look at the fire and say to himself, "hah! there could be other fires; let me poke around this smokey cavern to discover similar indoctrinations." It is not the first step toward relativism. The now-critical parolee rather looks at the fire with new wonder and respect, perhaps even awe. His expostulation would be more akin to this: "So this is the true origin and meaning of those wonderous tales of my youth!" It is the realization that the passing shadows of his indoctrination have an illuminative origin not discernible in the flickering shades on the wall that rivets him with new disclosure. He recognizes the shadows that he has grown to love are only images; the truth of them lies behind them. To be able to see the flame, always hurtful to the eyes, assures him not of the wrongness of his original learning, but merely of its derivative status. We may originally believe that promise keeping and truth telling should determine our conduct simply because our parents and then our community tell us so. But as we mature and learn the inherent rationality of such maxims, they become even more precious to us. This discovery is both cruel and comforting: we no longer can rely solely on the authority of our parents or community, and this is a painful loss of innocence for they then become less needful; but we are comforted and grateful because, in seeing their illuminative origin, we realize we were instructed rightly. Our grasp of the origins (as reasons) may now allow us to judge more acutely what our earlier instructions mean. We can never return to our original, trusting state, not because we now know what we believed is false but because we accept it critically, that is, with reasons rather than naively.

The first step of learning, in which what is seen is refined by becoming free to see the light that lets us see, is therefore not a discovery of new or different facts or even of new or different moral presuppositions. It is both amazing and arrogant that some contemporary interpreters of the myth see in this emancipation the mere realization that our first impressions on the wall are cast by the light of prejudice; that the first step toward self-refining learning is the realization that other people hold other religious or cultural views, and, hence, we must learn to step out of our culture and rank it as a mere possibility to be dispensed with or replaced at random. The Greeks, as well as most other societies both ancient and modern, were well aware that other people held other values. There is no profundity in this, nor is it the beginning of wisdom or even learning. It is something that both the wise and the foolish know, so knowing it is not what makes one wise; indeed, it is banal information. Somehow the realization that there are other cultural values has become a contemporary nostrum, a snake-oil remedy for all viral contagions of bigotry and superstition; but like all nostra, it deceives even as it fails to cure. Such juvenile reading is unworthy of the text.

There is a deep paradox here. The released prisoner, seeing the source of illumination, has a more profound grasp of what his former fellow-prisoners still see merely as shadows, but the very release that allows him to realize the greater truth cuts him off from the natural camaraderie of unreflective belonging. It is analogous to the great military commander whose mere presence on the field brings the troops together to fight splendidly as a unit, but who himself, as leader, is denied the warmth of friendship. Command isolates in utter loneliness even as it gathers together the warriors in that palpable, fierce intimacy unparalleled in human experience. The apprentice thinker, first released, is alien to his homeland in the very discovery of what makes the home his own; yet this discovery provides him with a superiority he cannot deny, a superiority that paradoxically links him with even greater authority to what is his own. He cannot ever go back. He has refined himself; or perhaps it is more accurate to say he has been refined by whatever lure (the love of learning) has wrenched him from the unreflective comfort of his own chains.

It is important to keep in mind that the released prisoner is not struck by the difference between the cutouts and the shadows, but rather that there is a fire. What we see is made available only because of a source of illumination other than what is usually thought to be seen. Strictly, I do not see the wrestler but the light waves that bounce off his glistening skin; it is the light that causes vision, not the object seen. This discovery troubles sharply. What is a wrestler except an image illuminated by something other than itself? The fire by itself does not suffice to cast the shadows; the light that reveals the wrestler is not the wrestler. Since the light is necessary to see the wrestler at all, however, it seems we are unable to confront the wrestler directly. What can be seen directly? The pain guides us: we can look at the fire. It does not hurt the eyes to look at the cutouts, but only to look directly at what illumines both the cutouts and their shadows: the fire itself.

This metaphor, as we noted earlier, strikes a deep resonance in us, even among those who are not particularly inclined to speculative thought. The disputes occur in the details. What does it mean to speak of this kind of learning? To the more analytic mind, it may simply provoke a restatement of the role mathematical science has in the check of raw, ungoverned experience: we all know slippery cups can fall and break; but the lover of learning realizes the causes that have mathematical formulae as their expression—soapy film makes it difficult to hold the cup, and gravity is expressed in precise equations. The more poetic mind sees in the same metaphor not scientific causes but principles that reveal fundamental essences: we all know we are going to die but Hamlet's soliloquy shows us how to think about it. Perhaps both are right, as long as neither claims exclusivity. In both readings the realization is made that to see the reason or the essence is something quite different than to see the mere event, and the former is as a light to shadow. Learning then proceeds from what is simply apprehended to what makes the apprehension possible. This learning is a refinement that frees us from the bondage of nonreflection; but this is not yet philosophy.

If the first stage of the prisoner's release provides an almost universal sympathy from readers, the second stage, when thought about, provides almost universal puzzlement. For if the apprentice learner sees that fires, and not objects or shadows, enlighten and hence refine, what could possibly be gained by the tedious trek outside the cave where a simply brighter fire, the sun, casts its shadows and illumines its objects? In this second stage or refinement, ordinary words become shibboleths. They are not things we know and can use to tell a story, they are things we do not know and, at best, we rely on the story to tell us what they mean. But this is entirely backward from ordinary intelligibility, and we must proceed with utmost caution. The most dangerous word in all of human discourse is "real," particularly in the realm of speculative thinking, where many sages crawl as refugees from the obvious. The learner is forced outside the cave where the "real" fire, the sun, illumines "real" objects, not cutout copies. We may think we know what it means to say such things, but reflection embarrasses this confidence and mocks the trust in our readiness. We forget, perhaps, the myth-teller's insistence that this is the most painful step of all. The original, chained prisoners, we recall, are sustained by the "false" food they see and are warmed by the "false" clothes they wear. But if food provides nutrition how can it be false? If the real food, cast by the true light of the sun, also provides nutrition, have we not lost a word or a pair of words, entirely? We cannot take refuge in appeals to causes, reasons, logical accounts and essential meanings since these are the benefits of the prisoner's first release inside the cave. So what, if anything, is gained in the exodus beyond the cave? A distinction is gained that has no meaning, it seems: the so-called difference between the fake and the real that makes no difference. Real is really an illusion.

Though Plato's myth must trouble us, we cannot thereby dismiss it. We must endure the pain and try again, perhaps with an analogy. Why have courage? we ask. The world would be a far more peaceful place if courage were excised entirely and all lived as cowards in tranquil acceptance of each other's rights. Plato himself, in the dialogue we are now considering, realizes there are grave and obvious dangers in the development and training of the courageous warrior class. However, we recognize that an unguarded state is a vulnerable state, and any excellence achieved in it will lure usurpatory predators, so that defenders are needed who must develop courage if they are to succeed. Courage, then, becomes a virtue, but it is a virtue with mere extrinsic value; we seek to become courageous for the sake of piety. That is, because we love what is our own, we must learn to sacrifice our own private interests and even lives for the community as a whole that makes our lives worth living. If there were no enemies, we would not need courage.

But we pause at this. Is this too glib? Perhaps, in some way difficult to pinpoint or explain, we might want to say that just being courageous is itself worthwhile. Perhaps, in other words, courage has intrinsic worth just as beauty does, and possibly the love of truth. Why would we say this? It may be that the training of the warrior in the craft of courage ennobles him, makes him beautiful in his youthful grace and strength, so that we would say: even if there were no wars we would admire courage just as courage. Life without courage is measured entirely by its length, but with it, life itself is the measure. The danger here is imminent: it is so facile to justify courage before some practical tribunal, as we seem to do with everything else, as those who are chained to see only shadows do. It takes courage to rank courage above its practical use. It takes courage to pray for courage. It takes courage to say it is worthwhile being courageous.

Outside the cave, we are told, is the only place the virtue of wisdom itself flourishes unfettered to service of the state. It is where philosophers only are allowed. To love truth simply because it is true and courage simply because it is courage is to love wisdom. The most dangerous word, "real," is here courageously realized. We need not justify truth—that is, make it just—we need only verify it—that is, make it true. What we see outside the cave is real only because it is true. This is what real must mean. The real, Socrates says earlier in the dialogue, is the ground of the true. Nothing else. So real depends on true; we do not love the real but the truth.

The myth of the cave is not about metaphysics but about learning. It explains what it means to educate the natural lover of learning—philomathes—to the unnatural lover of truth for its own sake—philosophes. If courage can, in the rarity of true thought, be seen as intrinsically worthwhile, so too can the love of truth. This is not a natural disposition, but one achieved only through the guildry of learning. It is refinement.

The myth does not end with a triumph but with a paradox. We learn the released prisoner is still not quite free. This in itself should disturb us greatly, for we are led by the myth to believe that it is truth that sets us free; yet this freest of all, this lover of the free and the true, is in deepest bondage. Painfully, unwillingly, unfreely, unjustly, he is brought back to the fuliginous murk of the cave where he can scarce distinguish anything at all. Why? To educate, and thereby hazard his life? The cruelest paradox is here: only the lover of truth for its own sake can be a true ruler in the one place where his wisdom is useless.

If we are stunnable at all, this must stun us most. What good is useless wisdom? Even to ask the question teaches: if good is utility the answer must be nothing. Useless wisdom is useless. The prisoner must return to the cave not because he will succeed, but because what he learns out there by the light of the sun is himself, not as a rarified mystic but as a historical, suffering lover of truth. For the sun outside the cave cannot be looked at directly, and, hence, our own questing becomes the object of the quest. Plato is in deep torment here—or rather, Socrates in the drama of learning is in torment. As early as the dialogue *Meno* he had suggested that perhaps knowledge was achievable by the simple, rational techniques of discovering the rules and principles of the mind, as the non-Athenian slave-boy seems to achieve by Socratic probing. If this is true, if all minds have latent within them the universal truths, then what need have we of Athenian culture, religion, and law? Anytus hears this and warns Socrates he is in danger of impiety. Perhaps he is, as his anguished questioning with Euthyphro suggests. But in the revisitation of these troubling issues in the *Republic*, the drama unfolds all of its exquisite paradox and torment. The warrior's training to love what is his own even beyond his own life is necessary for the thinker most of all. The wise rulers are chosen only from among the piously and courageously trained warriors. Why? It is not because we might be able to discover, by "pure reason," the rules of geometry, for we do not need courage for this. It is because true wisdom reveals us, and we are historical and pious in our denuding self-discovery.

The myth suggests this. Our very perceptions can be refined, not merely to see plain objects more plainly but to see and learn, even as perceivers, our own refinement. This refinement, as we have learned, is not of the disdainful elite who scorn the common, but of the learning itself, which surpasses even as it enriches our own commonality. Only if there is truth, and not mere opinion, is the refinement of learning possible. The best way to educate, Socrates tells us earlier in the dialogue, is to point out beauty to the youth at every opportunity so that, as he learns, he will greet reason as an old friend with whom he has long been acquainted. He then makes the great analogy between the two kinds of education: the gymnastic, in which the naked body is made beautiful, and music, in which the naked soul is made beautiful. The term here is *Kalon*, the noble. Learning makes us noble: it refines, and courage is essential for this refinement.

Throughout the genealogy of this learning each step has taken place by force. This makes sense to us because the comfort and satisfaction found in the various stages could not be overcome without the provocation of an allure that leads us through the pain of the exodus. We now realize that the forceful guide whose violence alone can bring us both beyond and then back into the cave is the love of learning itself. It might possibly indicate the teacher; but if so, it is not an external being possessed of knowledge but a colearner who leads the youth to self-learning. The return to the cave is often interpreted as some extraphilosophical duty to the state, for Socrates does say the now-philosopher would rather stay outside. The reluctance to move is a characteristic of every stage of the refinement. If wisdom be a virtue, it must make us noble; the beauty that leads us painfully out of the cave is the same that leads us back in: the beauty of truth itself. The learner, in learning, learns to share the truth with those who are his own. This is the ultimate response to the self-inflicted drama of critique against Socrates's putative impiety in the *Euthyphro*. Piety is not piety unless it questions itself and then questions its own questioning. Perhaps the cave-myth is but an echo of the purest dramatist's wisdom: Aeschylus teaches us, if he teaches anything, that only through suffering are we made wise. The philosopher suffers in returning; however, the return is not external to philosophy but internal. Socrates still offers sacrifices to the gods and will not seek exile outside of Athens—not because of some misplaced emotional attachment for a place, but because the true philosopher must also be both courageous and pious. It is, to be sure, an examined piety rather than a naive one. The youth is taught not to see new flowers but to see the beauty in those already there. Learning does not place us beyond the world, but simply shows us what it means to be in the world—an endless, painful, wonder-bestowing education, linking courage with beauty. It refines who we are; it does not inform us of secrets known only to initiates. Since education refines who we are, the return inherent in the drama is inevitable, just as Oedipus's discovery of his fearsome truth is inevitable given his noble and truth-revering character. The return to the cave is thus analogous to Oedipus's return to Thebes. It is an essential part of being a philosopher, not an externalist political misfortune. To refine who we are is not to put on new guises, but to learn who we really are; the fine can have no contempt for our common and shared place, nor find in exile from where we belong any solace or comfort. That this wisdom conflicts with the conceptual model of mind as formal unifier, distorted by Enlightenment metaphysics and the distraction of swelling technological advance is neither surprising nor new. Only its truth matters, not its pedigree. To realize truth matters independently is rare and tough; it is also redemptive.

Perhaps we should learn from these reflections to guard against the superstitions of our day, for overcoming superstition is essential for refinement. That the fine itself is the antidote to the virus of nihilism and superstition may be as difficult for us to grasp as it is difficult for the prisoner to find his way out of the cave and then back into it. The vulgar and the isolationist elite are both links in the chain that binds. Our children are being fettered to look at shadows only when they are taught opinions matter rather than truth. The modern superstitions, that the young are instinctively good, that refinement is mere snobbishness, that the vulgar is somehow honest or even fun are all cruel dissembling. It is crass superstition to believe all values are equal, yet we seem to propagate this illusion like dangerous mothers stuffing cream puffs into obese children. We confuse gratification with pleasure, pleasure with happiness, happiness with worth, worth with value, value with feelings, feelings with liberty, and liberty with license. We have, in these confusions, made children into murderers, whores, addicts, suicides, sexual wantons, nihilists, wretches, and orphans even in their own homes. There is so little refinement, so much vulgarity, so little integrity, and so much emptiness.

Yet this grim listing of social ills itself seems almost an indulgence. It is so facile to whine at the state of wretchedness. Perhaps such lamentation is unfit for philosophical discourse. The prisoner must, to be sure, return to the cave; but the thinker is not primarily a social critic. It is enough briefly to acknowledge these very real ills. The language of social malaise itself, however, distracts. We must seek to refine ourselves first; the refining of others must be a consequence of this. It is not social engineering but philosophical truth seeking that matters. The fine matters. But the young are apprentices and cannot flourish outside the guild. That this is true, and not mere opinion, itself is made available by the quest for the fine.

Index

achieved indifference, 71, 72
Aeschylus, 146–47, 155
aesthetics: aesthetic judgments as reflective, 131; aesthetic toughness, 47–48; of the fine, 37–48; morality distinguished from, 63; refinement beginning aesthetically, 63; revulsion of sameness, 83. *See also* art; beautiful, the
agency, 58
Antigone, 101, 146
Antony and Cleopatra (Shakespeare), xi, xii, xiii, 42, 58
Aquinas, Thomas, 10
architecture, 13–14, 51
Aristotle, 10
art: appealing to both the crowd and the few, 84; architecture, 13–14, 51; authority of, 14–15, 108–9, 110; conceptual art as elitist, 85; as cultural mirror, 51; enabled reception in, 13–17; enabling by submission to perception, 14; great artists as refining and perfecting, 21–22; immortalizing mortality, 43; judged by fineness by which it reveals its theme, 44–45; learning through, 13–14; making us who we are, 50; Michelangelo, 22, 64, 100; mysteries of our being revealed in, 100; natural beauty contrasted with, 11, 48; overemphasizing the conceptual or emotional elements, 85; perfection in, 3, 69; as play, 103; popular art as vulgar, 85; as probing toward essence, 51; sciences distinguished from, 101; tough art, 47–48; truth revealed by, 103, 110; universality of, 130–31. *See also* aesthetics; drama; music; painting; poetry
As You Like It (Shakespeare), 47, 65–67, 70, 73–74, 110
Auden, W. H., 2, 105, 108–9, 110
authority: of art, 14–15, 108–9, 110; compelling through legitimacy, 109, 111; in essences, 27–28; the fine as authoritative, 111–12; of the law, 131–32; in learning, 20; making possible as true meaning of, 24; no longer relying on that of our parents, 149; in perception, 8, 14; philosophy as inconsistent with, 148; power distinguished from, 20, 131; submission to, 25; of truth, 20, 111; universal authority, 128; of the welcome home, 27, 110

beautiful, the (beauty): Aquinas on, 10; beauty as refined elegance, xiii; as the concrete raised to the universal, 70; the fine as, xiii, 3, 65; grace as duty done beautifully, 67, 68; Kant on, 10; natural beauty contrasted with art, 11,

48; as not always good, 63, 64, 70; perception's meaning revealed by, 12; as philosophical significance of refinement, 24; Plato on, 10; as pleasing the senses, 10–13; submission to thrall of, 6; worth of, 70, 72
becoming who we are: as ground of meaning, 112; learning as, 52, 55–57, 98–99, 103, 109, 135; not that we become but what we become, 111; as ontological basis of the fine, 113; as our reality, 112–13
Beethoven, Ludwig van, 100, 108
belief. *See* opinion
Blake, William, 14

Cain, 121
Cassandra, 147
character, 58–60; essence and, 59, 60; etiquette and refinement of, 68; meaning and, 59, 60
chiding, 73–74
Cleopatra, xi, xii, xiii, 42, 58
comedy, 106, 109
common, the, 79–88; adherence to as unworthy, 82; elitist disdain for, 79, 81, 82, 106, 140; the fine contrasted with, 115; the fine entailing contempt for, 83, 122; the fine transforming, 106, 122; holding the dear at expense of the precious, 86–88; as minimal conditions for humanity, 80–81; rejection of as not elitist, 82–83, 122; unsurprising existence as, 110; as vulgar, 82, 83. *See also* vulgarity
courage, 83, 86–88, 152, 155
crass, the, 115
crude, the, 47–48
cultural difference, 149–50

dandyism, 29–30
dear, the, 83–84, 85–88
Death of a Salesman (Miller), 60

deconstructionists, 133
Descartes, René, 23
dialectical thinking, 93
Dickinson, Emily, 1–2, 3, 4, 8, 28, 137
divine providence, 57
drama: comedy, 106, 109; *Death of a Salesman*, 60; dramatic conflict in search for wisdom, 145; dramatic element in Platonic dialogues, 145–48; *Pygmalion*, 49–50, 62. *See also* Shakespeare, William; tragedy
duty, 67, 68

education: musical-gymnastic education, 50, 154; Plato on, 101, 153–54; as refining, 155; and teaching, 62, 101–2. *See also* learning
elitism: the common disdained by, 79, 81, 82, 106, 140; conceptual art as elitist, 85; egalitarian argument used by, 82; the fine as not an elite, 122; pejorative ring to, 82; refinement dismissed as, 83; rejection of, 83; rejection of the common not, 82–83, 122; as vulgar, 82, 106, 140
"embraced surpassing," 41
equality, 61–62; egalitarian argument used by elitists, 82; egalitarian denial of greatness, 80; equal sameness as nihilist, xi; ideological egalitarianism, 73; inequality, 60; the vulgarian defense as egalitarian, 77
erotic bondage, 65
essences: art probing toward, 51; being inessential, 52–53; character and, 59, 60; confronting, 22–28; the fine as essential, xv; the fine revealing, xvi, 3; having an essence, 52; of a home, 27; as how we must think about something, 3; locus of, 23; of

Index

love, 28; as of meanings, 23, 27–28, 51; as necessary conditions for a concept, 23; not known as objects, 26; perceived essences, 19–36; perceiving without, 28–36; revealed in a word, 2; as synthesizing, 25–26; thought made possible through, 24, 27, 35, 53; truth of self-becoming as essence of the fine, 111; as underlying authority that provides meaning, 27–28; the vulgar as having no essence, 54
esthetes, 29–30
ethics. *See* morals
etiquette, 68, 89
Euripides, 146–47
excellent, the, xiii
exile, 27, 110, 117, 122, 155
explanations, 143
external world, 27

Faerie Queene, The (Spenser), 11, 108
fine, the: achieved partly by refinement, xii, 52; achieving unfolding as a story, 58; aesthetics of, 37–48; as antidote to nihilism, 155; art judged by fineness by which it reveals its theme, 44–45; as authoritative, 111–12; as beautiful, xiii, 3, 65; becoming fine, 49–62; becoming who we are as ontological basis of, 113; the common contrasted with, 115; the common transformed by, 106, 122; contempt for the common and, 83, 122; when corrupted, 63–64; the crass contrasted with, 115; as embraced surpassing, 41; equality of rights and, 62; essences revealed by, xvi, 3; as essential, xv; ethics of, 64, 65, 68; etymological origins of, xii; as exemplars, 123, 124; existence as proper realm of, 112; fine and garish love, 39–41, 44; fine language in poetry, 2–3; fine language revealing, xi, 44; fine perceiving achieved through refinement, 4; fine truth, 89–103; a fine young man, 61; finitude embraced by, 42–43; fully realized only when lost, xi, xiii, 42; the garish and, 38–39, 41, 42; the good and, xiii, 63, 65; grace as, 67, 75; graciousness concretizing, 70; joy of, 124–25; as judgmental, xv, xvi, 137; juries as, 123–24; as leading, 112, 125; meanings of, xii; morals transcended by, 122; multiple counterimages of, 115; as noble, xiii, 43; as not elitist, 122; as a perspective, 42; the philosopher as, 139–56; preference for, 124–25; as principled, 135; as the radiant, 103, 125; rank established by, 3; as refined, xiii; as revealing, 43; sacrifice and, 43; sameness contrasted with, xi, xii, xiii, xv, 79; as sharp and penetrative, 3; as simple, 84; sins of as sacrilege, 65; solidity of, 94–95; as sources of refinement, 123; speaking finely making us fine, 50; study of providing a methodology for philosophy, 141; submission to thrall of, 6; the tough as a dimension of, 45, 140; as triumphing over what makes us wretched, 119; truth of self-becoming as essence of, 111; as unifying phenomenon, xiii; the vulgar distinguished from, 106, 115; vulgarity transformed by, 106–7, 111–12; as the vulgar transformed, 109, 111–12; welcome radiated by, 103, 123, 125, 129; the wretched contrast-

ed with, 122–24, 139. *See also* refinement
I Corinthians (St. Paul), 127, 129
flattery, 74
folly, 93, 110
friendship, loss of, 120–22

garishness: as deceiving, 43; the fine and, 38–39, 41, 42; fine and garish love, 39–41, 44; finitude disregarded by, 42–43; as lacking refinement, 38; world bereft of sacrifice as, 43
gender, 71
Gettysburg Address, 21, 127–28, 129–30, 131, 136
glee, 103
good, the: ability to do, 76; the beautiful not always good, 63, 64, 70; being good and doing good, 69; the fine as, xiii, 63, 65; grace contrasted with, 67, 69; worth of, 70, 72
gracious, the (grace), 63–78; abundance and, 66–67; acting morally but ungraciously, 69; as a bestowal, 68–69; depicted in *As You Like It,* 65–67; as duty done beautifully, 67, 68; external manifestations of, 68; as fine, 67, 75; the fine concretized by, 70; as flattery, 74; goodness contrasted with, 67, 69; gratitude by recipient of, 68–69; as noble, 83; in overlap of the good and the beautiful, 70; scandal contrasted with, 67; as supererogatory, 67, 68; teaching what worth is, 75; as treating people as having worth, 70–71, 72; as welcoming, 74
gratitude: for bestowal of grace, 68–69; in reception, 6, 8
greatness, 80, 124
grief, 75
guilds, 99

Hamlet (Shakespeare), 115–18, 120, 147
health, 46
Heidegger, Martin, xiv, 7, 110
hermits, 105–7
heroes, 59–60, 122
home, 27, 110–11, 122
hope, 115
Hume, David, 5, 75

ignorance, 98, 100
individual, the, 136
inequality, 60
innocence, 107–8; loss of as we mature, 149; transforming, 108, 112; vulgarity of, 107; wonder and, 108; worth of, 107
interpreting a text, 133–34
Ismene, 146, 147

Jocasta, 146, 147
joy: as both earned and bestowed, 124–25; of the fine, 124–25; in learning, 102, 103; of truth, 103; of welcome, 102–3, 125
judges, 131–32, 134
judgment, 127–37; aesthetic judgments as reflective, 131; art judged by fineness by which it reveals its theme, 44–45; avoiding for sake of sameness, 53, 54; decision procedures contrasted with, 134; faculty of, 128; the fine as matter of, xv, xvi, 137; in interpreting a text, 133–34; judgmental learning, 134–35; laws as formally vacuous without, 134; lost in a mass, 81; as neither opinion nor certainty, xvi; the particular and the universal as problem of, 128, 134, 137; as refinement of the self, 135–36; as species of refinement, 137, 139; in statutory rape laws, 132–33; the universal and the individual gathered by,

136; welcome in, 135; worth as basis of, 71–72; the wretched as incapable of, 137, 139
juries, 123–24
justice, 68, 148

kalon, 154
kalos, xiii
Kant, Immanuel: on aesthetic judgments as reflective, 131; on the beautiful and the good, 64, 70; on beauty, 10; on judgment, 128, 134; on moral worth, 67, 69; on receptivity, 5; on the sublime as felt not reasoned, 81
Keats, John, 2, 43
King Lear (Shakespeare), 9–10, 47, 51, 117
knowledge: as after the fact, 96–97; ignorance outranked by, 98; learning as acquisition of, 96, 97–98; learning mattering more than, 139; love of, 103; opinion surpassed by, 96; our having just enough to realize we are cheated, 142; as propositional, 97; relativism, 3–4, 16, 90–91; self-discovery contrasted with, 102; skepticism, xiii, 72, 73, 90–91; as true belief, 95–96; truth as necessary condition for, 98; utility of, 111; wisdom contrasted with, 142

laws: authority of, 131–32; decided by courts, 131–32; formally vacuous without judgment, 134; judges, 131–32, 134; juries, 123–24; reified when judgment is dispensed with, 136; statutory rape laws, 132–33; universality of, 131
learning, 55–62; as acquisition of knowledge, 96, 97–98; as assimilation or as practice, 55; authority in, 20; as becoming who we are, 52, 55–57, 98–99, 103, 109, 135; the bitter and the sweet in, 102; depending on futurity, 99–100; as discovering truth, 20, 61; existential learning, 55, 57; first step of, 149; from history or our own mistakes, 99; from the wise, 134; how learning welcomes, 102–3; ignorance in, 100; joy in, 102, 103; judgmental learning, 134–35; knowing mattering less than, 139; lovers of compared to philosophers, 145, 153; myth of the cave as metaphor for, 145, 153; proceeding from apprehension to what makes apprehension possible, 151; as a process, 99; as a refinement, 137, 151, 154; second stage of, 151; as self-learning, 26–27, 111; as showing us what it means to be in the world, 155; as storylike unfolding, 56, 57; through art, 13–14; through perception, 8–9; transformation as, 107; true learning, 102. *See also* education
Lincoln, Abraham: authority of, 20–21; Gettysburg address, 21, 127–28, 129–30, 131, 136; life of, 60; showing what it means to be American, 23, 24, 25
literal interpreters of scripture, 133
lives, 59–61; inequality of, 60; of the saints, 59; without meaning, 53–54; as stories, 113
Locke, John, 5
love: as Christian virtue, 129; erotic bondage, 65; essence of, 28; fine and garish love, 39–41, 44; in Gertrude, 116; of knowledge, 103; loss of, 122; philosophy as love of wisdom, 144, 153; of truth for its own sake, 142–44, 153; the vulgar view of, 77

manners, good, 61, 68
masses, the: mob behavior in, 81–82; rejection by the refined, 83; as statistics, 79; as vulgar, 83
Master-Singers of Nuremburg, The (Wagner), xiii
mathematics, 101, 151
meaning: becoming who we are as ground of, 112; character and, 59, 60; defined, 23–24; essence as of, 23, 27–28, 51; lives without, 53–54; as measure of refinement, 51; in nihilism's refutation, 72–73; our reality as ground of, 113; refining making possible, 54
Michelangelo, 22, 64, 100
A Midsummer Night's Dream (Shakespeare), 93, 100
Miller, Arthur, 60
mirroring, 135, 136
morals (ethics): acting morally but ungraciously, 69; aesthetics distinguished from, 63; beyond morality, 119; duty, 67, 68; ethics of the fine, 64, 65, 68; the fine as transcending, 122; as the universal applied to the particular, 70; wretchedness transcending, 118–19. *See also* good, the; virtue
mortality: art immortalizes, 43; as a kindness, 1, 2, 4
Mozart, Wolfgang Amadeus: appealing to both the crowd and the few, 84; coarseness used by, 32; *Jupiter Symphony*, 16; perfection in, 3, 69, 110; music: Beethoven, 100, 108; coarse sounds used in, 32; learning what it means to hear through, 13; musical-gymnastic education, 50, 154; Verdi, 84. *See also* Mozart, Wolfgang Amadeus

Nietzsche, Friedrich, 54

nihilism: absence of the fine entailing, xiii–xiv; of equal sameness, xi, xii, xiii; the fine as antidote to, 155; meaningfulness of everything refuting, 72–73; the vulgar and, 77
noble, the: courage of, 86–87; the fine as, xiii, 43; the gracious as, 83; juries as, 124; *kalon,* 154; as paradoxical, 84; as a rarity, 79, 80; as sacrificial and courageous, 83–84, 86–88, 130; wisdom making us, 154

Oedipus, 146, 155
opinion: judgment as neither certainty nor, xvi; knowledge as true belief, 95–96; knowledge surpassing, 96; and orthodoxy, 95, 96, 103; tolerance of diversity of, 90; truth as distinct from, xiv, 70, 71, 95. *See also* philodoxy
Orestes, 146–47
orthodoxy, 95, 96, 103
Othello (Shakespeare), 147

painting: coarse depictions in, 32; learning what it means to see through, 13; Michelangelo's Sistine Chapel, 100; Rembrandt, 15, 16; van Gogh, 48
parents, 27, 123, 149
particulars and universals, 128, 131, 134, 137
Paul, Saint: *I Corinthians,* 127, 129; local advocacy of, 134–35; as vicar and mirror, 136
perception: authority inherent in, 8, 14; deliberate coarsening of, 31–36; enabled reception in art, 13–17; as enabling, 6, 7, 8–13; without essence, 28–36; fine perceiving achieved through refinement, 4; gratitude in reception, 6, 8; learning through,

8–9; meaning of, 4–8; meaning of revealed by the beautiful, 12; as not passive, xvii, 7; only of what is already there, 22; perceived essences, 19–36; perceiving our own perceiving, 10, 11; perceiving our own refinement, 154; perceiving well or badly, 15, 16, 34–35; pleasure in, 10–13; as reception, 5–8; refined, 1–17, 99; refining of, 15–16, 19–22, 139, 154; relativism in, 16; selectivity lacking in, 7–8; submission in, 6–7, 8–9, 14, 26, 31; *tabula rasa*, 5; thinking in, 4; utilitarian, 30–31; vulgar, 28. *See also* reception
perfection: in art, 3, 69, 110; great artists as perfecting not innovating, 21–22; relativism and, 4
philodoxy, 90–95; allures of, 93; glee in, 103; need for approval by the student leading to, 102; relativism and skepticism contrasted with, 90–91; as silly, 94; as vulgar, 89, 90, 94; as wanton, 92
philosophers: as courageous and pious, 155; distinctions made by, 105–6; as fine, 139–56; and lovers of learning, 145, 153; as lovers of wisdom, 144; as outside the cave, 153; philosophy as a refinement, 140; study of the fine providing a methodology for, 141; wonder required for philosophy, 107
Pietà (Michelangelo), 64
piety, 155
Plato: on beauty, 10; on courage, 83, 152; dramatic element in dialogues of, 145–48; on education, 101, 153–54; on knowledge as justified true opinion, 96; on musical–gymnastic education, 50, 154; myth of the cave, 144–45, 148–54; on perception as reception, 5; on reality as the most excellent, xiv; on reason as a carnival, 93; on relativism in perception, 16; on truth and opinion, xiv; on wisdom, 142
pleasure: in beauty, 10–13; as cause or motive, 12; in perception, 10–13; preference for the fine and, 124
poetry: Auden, 2, 105, 108–9, 110; Blake, 14; Dickinson, 1–2, 3, 4, 8, 28, 137; essence of love penetrated by, 28; fine language in, 2–3; Keats, 2, 43. *See also* Shakespeare, William
precious, the, 83–84, 85–88
principles, 134, 135
Pygmalion (Shaw), 49–50, 62

quests, the: advancement by refining the questioning, 19; as failing, 139–41; as its own object, 153; as needful, 141–42; as tentative, xiv; as transforming, 139–40; for truth, xv, 141

racism, 71
real, the, 151–52, 153
reality, 112–13
reason, 93, 109, 154
reception: enabled reception in art, 13–17; enabled by our receptivity, 8–13; gratitude in, 6, 8; perception as, 5–8; refinement of, 22. *See also* perception
refinement: as aesthetic and moral, 63; dismissed as elitism, 83; education as refining, 155; etiquette in refinement of character, 68; the fine achieved by, xii, 52; the fine as refined, xiii; the fine as sources of, 123; the garish as lacking in, 38; great artists as refining, 21–22; as improving what is already

given, 21–22; judgment as, 135–36, 137, 139; learning as a, 137, 151, 154; learning who we are only possible through, 98–99; meaning as measure of, 51; meaning made possible by, 54; misrepresented as stuffiness, 77; paradox of, 21–22; perceiving our own, 154; as philosophically significant, 24; philosophy as, 140; proceeding from vicarage to mirroring, 135; of receptivity, 22; refined perception, 1–17, 99; refining ourselves, 51, 156; refining perception, 4, 15–16, 19–22, 139, 154; as revealing the authority inherent in an essence, 27; as strengthening not decorative, 22; threefold reality and, 129; toughness and, 47; tragedy as refining our suffering into truth, 103; truth as, 100; truth established by, 129; utilitarian perception as threat to, 31; vulgarity not gainsaid by, 109
relativism, 3–4, 16, 90–91
religion: achieved indifference to, 71; divine providence, 57; hermits, 105–7; literal interpreters of scripture, 133; lives of the saints, 59; orthodoxy, 95, 96, 103; piety, 155; sacrifice, 43, 83, 86–88, 109, 121, 130; saints, 59–60, 106, 107. *See also* Paul, Saint
respect, 136
revulsion, 35, 83, 123
Richard II (Shakespeare), 127–28, 130–31, 141
Rogers, Will, xvi
Romeo and Juliet (Shakespeare), 37–45, 58
rudeness, 77

sacrifice, 43, 83, 86–88, 109, 121, 130

saints, 59–60, 106, 107
sameness: aesthetic revulsion of, 83; avoiding judgments for sake of, 53, 54; the fine contrasted with, xi, xii, xiii, xv, 79; as nihilistic, xi, xii, xiii
scandal, 63, 64, 67, 69
sciences, 101, 151
scolding, 73–74
self-criticism, 125
self-learning, 26–27, 111
self-loathing (self-hatred), 125, 129, 135
self-respect, 136
Shakespeare, William: appealing to both the few and the crowd, 84; comic plots of, 58; folly made endearing by, 93; as perfecting not innovating, 21; slave sonnets, 47; Sonnet Sixty-seven, 63, 69; Sonnet Ninety-four, 64. *See also under specific titles*
Shaw, George Bernard, 49–50, 62
silly, the, 93, 94
skepticism, xiii, 72, 73, 90–91
Socrates, 145–48, 155
Socratic method, 101
solecisms, 89
Sophocles, 101, 102, 146–47
statistics, 79
statutory rape, 132–33
stories, 57–58; character, 58–60; elements of, 58; inequality of, 60; learning as storylike, 56, 57; lives as, 113
submission: to authority, 25; to authority of art, 14–15; in perception, 6–7, 8–9, 14, 26, 31; to power, 25; to thrall of beauty and the fine, 6
surprise: in existence through art, 108–9, 110; as violence to expectation, 110–11

teaching and education, 62, 101–2
terrorism, 94

texts, interpretation of, 133–34
thinking: dialectical, 93; essence as how we must think about something, 3; "for themselves," 102; grounded in truth, 144; made possible through essence, 24, 27, 35, 53; muddled thinking as foe of the fine, xv; in perception, 4; reason, 93, 109, 154
tolerance, 90
tough, the, 45–48; crudeness distinguished from, 47–48; as dimension of the fine, 45, 140; refinement and, 47; tough art, 47–48
tragedy: Aeschylus, 146–47, 155; Euripides, 146–47; as refining our suffering into truth, 103; Sophocles, 101, 102, 146–47. *See also under specific character names*
transformation, 105–13; the common transformed by the fine, 106, 122; the fine as the vulgar transformed, 109, 111–12; of innocence, 108, 112; as learning, 107; quests as transforming, 139–40; as refinement, 107; of the self, 111–12; vulgarity transformed by the fine, 106–7, 111–12
truth: achieved indifference to, 71; art revealing, 103, 110; authority of, 20, 111; as earthly, 103; eloquence not invalidating, 128; fine truth, 89–103; as ground of virtue, 144; joy of, 103; knowledge as true opinion, 95–96; learning as discovering, 20, 61; learning who we are as, 98–99, 103, 109; learning from the wise, 134; loving for its own sake, 142–44, 153; muddled thinking as foe of, xv; never trite in philosophy, 140; as not consisting of answers, 142–43; opinion as distinct from, xiv, 70, 71, 95; personal advocacy as part of, 135; of propositions, 97; quest for, xv, 141; the real as ground of, 153; as refinement, 100, 129; in self-learning, 111; as solely a necessary condition for knowledge, 98; success not guaranteed by, 100; thought grounded in, 144; tolerance in service of, 90; tragedy as refining our suffering into, 103; universal truth, 127–28, 153; the vulgar disregard, 83, 84, 88, 89, 94; why search for, 141–42

universals: art, 130–31; beauty as the concrete raised to the universal, 70; laws, 131; morality as the universal applied to the particular, 70; particulars and, 128, 131, 134, 137; Paul's universal church, 129; universal authority, 128; universal truth, 127–28, 153

value, 70, 71, 149–50
van Gogh, Vincent, 48
Verdi, Giuseppe, 84
vicarage, 135, 136
vice, 144
virtue: courage as, 152; intrinsic worth of truth as ground of, 144; love as, 129; vice, 144; wisdom as, 142, 143, 144
vulgarity: aggressive harshness of, 77; the common, 82, 83; elitists, 82, 106, 140; esthetes, 29–30; the fine as the vulgar transformed, 109, 111–12; the fine distinguished from, 106, 115; for its own sake, 89; as having no essence, 54; as idleness or laziness, 84; of innocence, 107; irrationality of, 77; the masses,

83; nihilism and, 77; original vulgarity, 108–9, 110; philodoxy as, 89, 90, 94; popular art, 85; as a possibility, xvi; success and unsuccess regarded unequally by, 100; transformed by the fine, 106–7, 111–12; truth not regarded by the vulgar, 83, 84, 88, 89, 94; the vulgar as diminishing their own worth, 77; the vulgar as simplistic, 84; the vulgarian defense as egalitarian, 77; vulgar language, 33–34, 35; vulgar origins not gainsaid by refinement, 109; vulgar perception, 28; worth not recognized by the vulgar, 76–78, 83, 84, 88. *See also* common, the

Wagner, Richard, xiii

welcome: art as the authority that surprises by the unexpected, 110–11; the fine radiating, 103, 123, 125, 129; forgiving, 119; the gracious as welcoming, 74; home and, 27, 110; the joy of, 102–3, 125; in judgment, 135

wisdom: conflicting with mind as a formal unifier, 155; dramatic conflict in search for, 145; knowledge distinguished from, 142; making us noble, 154; philosophy as love of, 144; suffering making us wise, 155; as useless, 153; as a virtue, 142, 143, 144

wise, the, 134

Wittgenstein, Ludwig, 23

wonder, 107, 108, 143

worth, 70–77; adherence to the common as unworthy, 82; as basis of judgment, 71–72; of beauty and the good, 70, 72; graciousness as treating people as having, 70–71, 72; gracious treatment teaching what worth is, 75; of innocence, 107; intrinsic worth of truth as ground of virtue, 144; moral, 67, 69; value distinguished from, 70, 71; the vulgar diminishing their own, 77; the vulgar not recognizing, 76–78, 83, 84, 88

wretched, the, 115–25; censure and pity appropriate to, 117; etymology of, 117–18; feeling wretched, 120; the fine as triumphing over what makes us wretched, 119; the fine contrasted with, 122–24, 139; as guilty victims, 123; inanimate objects as, 119–20; as without judgment, 137, 139; juries as, 123–24; morality transcended by, 118–19; as self-induced, 122; self-loathing in, 125, 129; those dispossessed of love or friendship as, 122

About the Author

Michael Gelven is Presidential Research Professor in Philosophy at Northern Illinois University. A former Fulbright Scholar at Freiburg im Breisgau, Germany, he has published eight books that have been translated into several languages and many scholarly articles on an array of philosophical issues. Since 1966 he has made his home at DeKalb, Illinois, where he satisfies his passion for teaching and finding opportunity for opera, skiing, theatre, and attending the Chicago Symphony Orchestra.

Other books by Michael Gelven include *War and Existence* (1994), *Truth and Existence* (1991), *Why Me? A Philosophical Inquiry into Fate* (1991), *Spirit and Existence* (1990), *A Commentary on Heidegger's Being and Time* (rev. ed. 1989), and *Winter, Friendship and Guilt: The Sources of Self-Inquiry* (1974).